Every
Handbook

Exclusive Distributors:
Music Sales Corporation
257 Park Avenue South, New York, NY 10010 USA
Music Sales Limited
8/9 Frith Street, London W1V 5TZ England
Music Sales Pty. Limited
120 Rothschild Street, Rosebery, Sydney, NSW 2018, Australia

Copyright © 1984 by Amsco Publications,
A Division of Music Sales Corporation, New York, NY.

Order No. AM 37391
US International Standard Book Number: 0.8256.2339.1
UK International Standard Book Number: 0.7119.0608.4

Printed in the United States of America by
Vicks Lithograph and Printing Corporation

Amsco Publications
New York/London/Sydney

Rudiments
Rudiments
Rudiments
Rudiments
Rudiments
Rudiments
Rudiments
Rudiments
Rudiments
Rudiments
Rudiments
Rudiments
Rudiments
Rudiments
Rudiments
Rudiments
Rudiments
Rudiments
Rudiments
Rudiments
Rudiments
Rudiments

Rudiments

Basics

Pitch Names

There are seven letter names in the musical alphabet: A B C D E F G
These correspond to another system of pitchmaking called *solfège.*

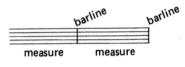

C	D	E	F	G	A	B
do	re	mi	fa	so	la	ti (or si)

Staff

Notes indicating specific pitches are written on the lines and
spaces of a five-line *staff.* *Barlines* divide the staff into equal
metrical units called *measures.*

Clefs

A *clef* appears at the beginning of each staff of music.
The *treble clef* is also known as the "G clef" because it circles the
line on which G above middle C is written.

The *bass clef* is also known as the "F clef" because it designates the
line on which F below middle C is written.

The treble and bass staves braced together are called the *grand staff.*

The various *C clefs* are so named because they designate middle C
wherever they are placed. The reason for the variable position of
this clef is to accommodate different vocal ranges.

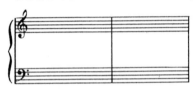

| soprano | mezzo-soprano | alto | tenor | baritone |

Leger Lines

Notes which occur above or below the staff are written on *leger lines*
small additional lines with the same line-space alternation.

Accidentals

There are twelve available tones within the octave in the western
music system. These are derived by the use of *accidentals,* symbols
which alter the pitch of one of the seven given letter-names.
A *flat* (♭) lowers the pitch by one half-step.
A *sharp* (♯) raises the pitch by one half-step.
A *natural* (♮) cancels any previous accidental, returning the pitch to
its unaltered state.
A *double flat* (♭♭) or *double sharp* (♯♯) alters the pitch by two
half-steps (one whole-step).

Enharmonics

Two notes which sound the same but are spelled differently are
enharmonic.

| A♯ /B♭ | F♭ /E |

Steps

The *half-step* (*semitone*) is the smallest intervallic unit in western
music. Two half-steps give us a *whole step* (*tone*).

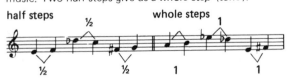

Scales

A *scale* is any consecutive arrangement of pitches.

Chromatic Scale

All twelve tones arranged in consecutive upward or downward half-step order are known as the *chromatic scale.* Usually sharps are used ascending, flats descending.

Diatonic Scales

A *diatonic scale* is an arrangement of consecutive half- and whole-steps in alphabetical sequence, using all seven letter-names. The particular pattern of steps determines the type of scale and remains consistent from octave to octave. There are two diatonic scales in common use: major and minor.

Major Scale

A *major scale* is a series of eight tones (the eighth being the octave repetition of the first) in which the pattern of half- and whole-steps is as follows:

C Major scale

Regardless of what tone the scale begins on, the pattern of half- and whole-steps is always the same.

Minor Scale

A *minor scale* is a series of eight tones which is characterized by the consistent appearance of a half-step between the second and third degrees. There are three forms of the minor scale.
The *natural minor* (*pure minor*):

The *harmonic minor scale* is similar to the natural minor except that the seventh degree is raised, resulting in a 1½-step gap between the sixth and seventh degrees.

The *melodic minor scale* has two forms: ascending and descending. The ascending form contains raised sixth and seventh degrees.

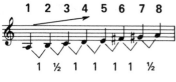

The descending form of the melodic minor scale is the same as the natural minor.

Modes

The precursor of the major and minor diatonic scales was a system of seven *modes* which originated in ancient Greece. Still in use today (mostly in folk and modern music) the modes are derived by beginning an octave scale on each degree of a C Major scale. The seven modes and their half- and whole- step patterns are as follows.

Modes

Ionian
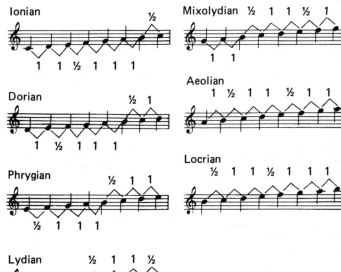

Mixolydian

Dorian

Aeolian

Phrygian

Locrian

Lydian

Scale Degree Names

1	**tonic** (determines the key or tonality)
2	**supertonic** ("super" = above)
3	**mediant** (midway between tonic and dominant)
4	**subdominant** ("sub" = below)
5	**dominant** (second only to tonic in importance)
6	**submediant** (midway between tonic and subdominant)
7	**leading tone** (back to tonic)

scale degrees in C Major

tonic   supertonic mediant subdominant dominant

submediant leading tone tonic

Whole-Tone Scale

A scale made up of only six members at whole-step intervals is called a *whole-tone scale.* There are only two possible whole-tone scales: on C and C♯.

Pentatonic Scales

Any scale consisting of only five members is called *pentatonic* (from the Greek "penta" meaning five). There are two types: tonal and semitonal. The *tonal pentatonic scale* contains no half-steps, only intervals of a whole-step or larger.

The *semitonal pentatonic scale* contains half-steps.

Keys

Key Signatures

With the exception of C Major and A minor, all keys must use one or more accidentals. To facilitate reading, the sharps or flats needed for a particular key appear at the beginning of each staff, giving us the *key signature*.

Major Keys

Keys requiring sharps are found in intervals of consecutive upward fifths. Each successive sharp key adds another sharp to the key signature. This new sharp is always the leading tone of the new key.

Keys requiring flats are found in intervals of consecutive downward fifths. Each successive flat key adds another flat to the key signature. This new flat is always the subdominant of the new key.

The major keys and their sharps and flats are as follows.

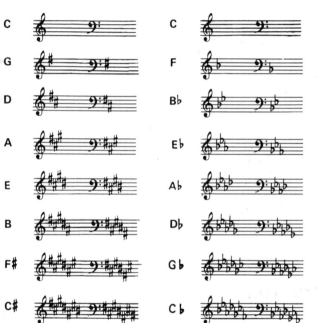

Minor Keys

A *minor key* has the same key signature as the major key which lies a minor third above it. For example, A minor has the same key signature as C Major (no sharps or flats).

The minor keys and their sharps and flats are as follows.

Relative Keys

A major key and a minor key which have the same key signature are known as *relative keys.* For example, A minor is the relative minor of C Major, and C Major is the relative major of A minor.

Parallel Keys

A major key and a minor key which have the same letter name are known as *parallel keys.* For example, G Major is the parallel key of G minor.

Enharmonic Keys

Two keys which sound the same but are spelled differently are termed *enharmonic.* There are three such pairs of enharmonic major keys.

Enharmonic major	Enharmonic minor
C♯ / D♭	B♭ / A♯
F♯ / G♭	E♭ / D♯
B / C♭	A♭ / G♯

Circle of Fifths

All the keys and their enharmonic relationships can be shown on the *circle of fifths,* an arrangement of the twelve keys so that the number of sharps in the key signature increases clockwise, and the number of flats counterclockwise.

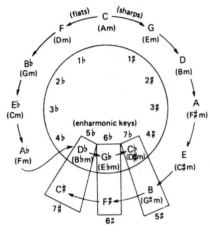

Intervals

An *interval* is the distance between two pitches. It is labelled according to the number of letter names it encompasses, counting both the first and last. For example, from C up to G is a "fifth" because it encompasses five letter names: C D E F G.

intervals on C

prime   2nd   3rd   4th   5th   6th   7th   octave
(unison)

A *melodic interval* occurs sequentially while a *harmonic interval* occurs simultaneously.

melodic interval   harmonic interval

5th

Interval Quality

Intervals can be *perfect, major, minor, augmented,* or *diminished.* The quality of an interval is determined by comparing the upper pitch to the major scale constructed on the lower pitch. If the upper pitch is within the major scale built on the lower pitch and it is a prime (unison), fourth, fifth, or octave, the interval is called *perfect* (P).

perfect intervals in C Major

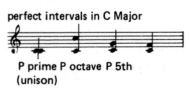

P prime   P octave   P 5th
(unison)

If the upper pitch is within the major scale built on the lower pitch and it is a second, third, sixth, or seventh, the interval is called *major* (M).

major intervals in C Major

M2nd   M3rd   M6th   M7th

If the upper pitch is not within the major scale built on the lower pitch, the following rules apply:
A major interval contracted a half-step is called *minor* (m).

M3rd m3rd

A major or perfect interval expanded a half-step is called *aug mented* (aug).

M3rd aug3rd   P5th aug 5th

A minor or perfect interval contracted a half-step is called *di minished* (dim).

m3rd dim3rd   P5th dim5th

Compound intervals are those which extend above the octave. Their qualities are the same as those of corresponding simple intervals (without the octave addition). For example, a minor ninth = octave + minor second; a major ninth = octave + major second, etc.

M9th   M10th

Interval Spelling

Regardless of the actual sound of an interval, it is *always* labelled according to the number of letter names it spans. For example, from C♯ down to E♭ is an augmented sixth although it sounds the same as the minor seventh C♯ down to D♯. Similarly, from C♯ up to D♭ is a diminished second although it sounds the same as the perfect prime C♯ / C♯.

aug 6th   P prime

Interval Inversions

When the top member of an interval is displaced to the octave below the bottom member (or vice versa), the interval is said to be *inverted*. The total number of the original interval (simple) and its inversion is always 9. For example, the inversion of a third is a sixth; the inversion of a fourth is a fifth, etc. The quality is inverted as well, so that the inversion is the opposite quality. For example, a major third becomes a minor sixth; a diminished seventh becomes an augmented second, etc.
Note: The inversion of a perfect interval is always another perfect interval.

inversions

M3rd m6th   m2nd M7th   P4th P5th dim 3rd aug 6th

Tritone

The augmented fourth (or diminished fifth) is called the *tritone* because it encompasses three whole-steps. In medieval music this interval was termed *diabolus in musica* (Latin, "the devil in music") because its extreme dissonance tends to destroy an established tonal focus.

1   1   1   tritone
                (aug 4th/dim 5th)

Chords

A *chord* is a simultaneous sounding of three or more pitches. In traditional harmony, all chords are constructed on a system of *superimposed thirds.*

A *triad* (three-note chord) is made up of the first, third, and fifth degrees of a scale. The first degree is the root of the triad and as long as it is the lowest note the triad is said to be in *root position.*

C Major

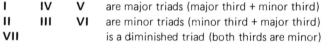

1   3   5   triad
(root)   (root position)

Chord Quality

Chords may be *major, minor, augmented,* or *diminished* according to their construction. When a triad is built on each degree of a major scale the qualities are as follows:

I	IV	V	are major triads (major third + minor third)
II	III	VI	are minor triads (minor third + major third)
VII			is a diminished triad (both thirds are minor)

C Major triad qualities

When a triad is built on each degree of a natural minor scale the qualities are as follows:

I	IV	V	are minor triads (minor third + major third)
III	VI	VII	are major triads (major third + minor third)
II			is a diminished triad (both thirds are minor)

A minor triad qualities

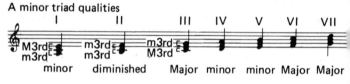

Higher-Number Chords

Chords of four or more members are termed *higher-number chords* and are named according to the highest interval (in root position). A *seventh chord* adds the seventh degree of the scale above the basic triad.

C Major

1   3   5   7   7th chord
(root)   (root position)

A *ninth chord* adds the ninth degree above the basic triad with seventh.

C Major

1   3   5   7   9   9th chord
(root)   (root position)

All further higher-number chords (elevenths, thirteenths, etc.) are derived in the same manner.

Dominant Chords

A major triad built on the fifth degree of the scale with a minor seventh added is a *dominant seventh* chord. Its harmonic function is to resolve to the tonic triad.

C Major
V7⎯⎯⎯→ I

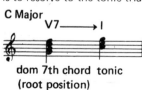

dom 7th chord tonic
(root position)

A dominant seventh chord with a ninth (major or minor) added is a *dominant ninth chord* and has the same harmonic function as a dominant seventh chord.

C Major

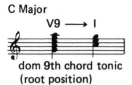

dom 9th chord tonic
(root position)

Chord Inversion

Any chord is said to be in *root position* as long as the root is the lowest note, regardless of the position of the other chord members. Whenever a chord-member other than the root is on the bottom, the chord is *inverted.*
If the third is on the bottom, the chord is in *first inversion.*
If the fifth is on the bottom, the chord is in *second inversion.*

triad inversion

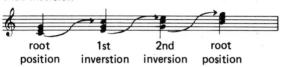

root   1st   2nd   root
position   inverstion   inversion   position

Higher-number chords have further inversions according to the number of chord members.

7th chord inversion

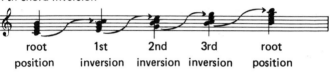

root   1st   2nd   3rd   root
position   inversion   inversion   inversion   position

Cadences

The most important chords in any key are I (tonic) and V (dominant) and IV (subdominant). The I and V chords are the primary elements of a *cadence,* a progression which established a particular key center (tonality) and ends a piece or section of a piece. A *perfect authentic cadence* is V followed by I with both the soprano and bass voices ending on the tonic. (Note: The cadential V chord is always major, even in a minor key.)

perfect authentic cadence

An *imperfect authentic cadence* is the same as a perfect authentic cadence except that the soprano voice ends on the third or fifth of the tonic chord (the bass is still on the tonic).

imperfect authentic cadence

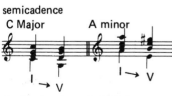

A *semicadence* is half an authentic cadence, pausing on the V chord instead of resolving to the tonic. A semicadence usually appears at the end of a phrase which is followed by another phrase ending with an authentic cadence.

semicadence

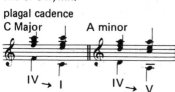

A *plagal cadence* is IV followed by I. This is less common than the authentic cadence and is often heard as the "Amen" chords at the end of a hymn.

plagal cadence
C Major   A minor

IV → I   IV → V

Time

Rhythm

Rhythm is the grouping of strong and weak beats, encompassing the elements of *pulse, accent,* and *subdivision*.

Dots

A dot beside a notehead lengthens the duration of the note by half its original value. (A second dot adds half the time of the first dot.)

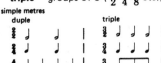

Time Signature

The *time signature* which appears beside the clef at the beginning of each piece or movement of music indicates the metre of the piece.

    top number = number of beats in each measure
    bottom number = note value which is the beat-unit

Thus a $\frac{3}{4}$ time signature means there are three quarter-note beats per measure. Other time signature notations are as follows.

$\mathbf{C}$ = $\frac{4}{4}$ (or *"common time"*)

$\mathbf{\Phi}$ = $\frac{2}{2}$ or *alla breve* (or *"cut time"*)

Metre

Metre is the regular grouping of beats into measures. There are two types of *simple metre.*

duple — groups of 2 or multiples of 2 ($\frac{2}{2}$ $\frac{2}{4}$ $\frac{2}{8}$ $\frac{4}{4}$ $\frac{4}{8}$ etc.)

triple — groups of 3 ($\frac{3}{2}$ $\frac{3}{4}$ $\frac{3}{8}$ etc.)

Compound Metre

Whereas the beats in simple metre are values subdivisible by two, the beats in compound metre are dotted values subdivisible by three.

compound duple — groups of 2 (or multiples of 2) dotted values, subdivisible by 3 ($\frac{6}{4}$ $\frac{6}{8}$ $\frac{12}{4}$ $\frac{12}{8}$ etc.)

compound triple — groups of 3 dotted values ($\frac{9}{4}$ $\frac{9}{8}$ etc.)

Composite Metre

Irregular groupings containing a mixture a duple and triple metres are called *composite* (or *added*) *metres.* For example, $\frac{5}{4} = \frac{2}{4} + \frac{3}{4}$ or $\frac{3}{4} + \frac{2}{4}$, $\frac{7}{8} = \frac{4}{8} + \frac{3}{8}$ or $\frac{3}{8} + \frac{4}{8}$, etc. Composite metres may also appear with alternative time-signatures.

Triplets

Three notes of equal duration which take up the same total time as two notes of the same written value constitute a *triplet*. This is indicated with a *3* over the triplet figure.

Tempo

The rate of speed of the music (whatever the metre) is called the *tempo.* There is usually a tempo indication at the beginning of each piece; traditionally in Italian but sometimes in German, French, or English.

Often there is a *metronome marking* instead of (or along with) the tempo indication. A metronome marking of *60* means that one tick = one second. Therefore, a marking of $\quad \downarrow = \mathbf{120}$ means that each quarter-note beat is represented by a half-second tick. Some standard tempo markings with their metronomical equivalents follow:

Largo 40-60 **Adagio** 66-76 **Moderato** 108-120 **Presto** 168-200

Larghetto 60-66 **Andante** 76-108 **Allegro** 120-168 **Prestissimo** 200-208

Notation

Stems

Stems extend upward from the right side of the notehead for notes on the middle line of the staff and below. Stems extend downward from the left side of the notehead for notes on the middle line of the staff or above.

Flags

Flags always appear to the right of the stem.

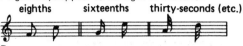

Beams

All notes belonging to a beat are beamed together, regardless of individual value.

Phrases/Slurs/Ties

A long curved line over a number of notes indicates a *phrase.*

 phrase

A curved line between two notes (or sometimes three) of *different pitch* is a *slur* (actually a smaller phrasing indication).

A curved line between two notes of the *same pitch* is a *tie.* The second note does not receive a new attack—its duration is added to that of the first.

Double Bars

A light double bar indicates the end of a section within a piece; a heavy double bar indicates the end of a piece or movement.

light double bar   heavy double bar

Repeat Signs

A dotted double bar means to repeat what appears between the beginning of the piece and the repeat sign. Two dotted double bars mean to repeat the passage between the two signs.

First and Second Endings

The first ending is played the first time through the passage; when the passage is repeated the first ending is skipped and the second ending is played instead.

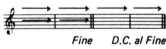

Da Capo

A simple *D.C.* or *Da Capo* means to repeat the section from the beginning. *Da Capo al Fine (D.C. al Fine)* means to return to the beginning of the piece and play to the indicated end *(Fine).* When playing a *D.C.,* repeats are not taken and first endings are skipped.

Fine   D.C. al Fine

Dal Segno

A simple *D.S.* or *Dal Segno* means to repeat from the sign (𝄋). *Dal Segno al Fine (D.S. al Fine)* means to return to the sign (𝄋) and play to the indicated end *(Fine).* When playing a *D.S.,* repeats are not taken and first endings are skipped.

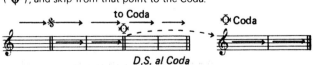

D.S.

D.S. Al Coda

A *D.S. al Coda* means to repeat from the sign (𝄋), play to the Coda sign (⊕), and skip from that point to the Coda.

to Coda   Coda

D.S. al Coda

Harmony
Harmony
Harmony
Harmony
Harmony
Harmony
Harmony
Harmony
Harmony
Harmony
Harmony
Harmony
Harmony
Harmony
Harmony
Harmony
Harmony
Harmony
Harmony
Harmony
Harmony
Harmony

Harmony
Harmony
Harmony
Harmony
Harmony
Harmony
Harmony
Harmony
Harmony
Harmony
Harmony
Harmony
Harmony
Harmony
Harmony
Harmony
Harmony
Harmony
Harmony
Harmony
Harmony
Harmony
Harmony

Definitions

Harmony: A combination of simultaneous tones, a musical system applied to combining simultaneous tones.

Functional harmony: the harmonic system used in Western music from the 17th century to the 20th century; a harmonic language based on the realtionship between triads of the major and minor scales.

Triad: A chord of three notes constructed of superimposed 3rds: the 1st (root), 3rd, and 5th degrees of a scale.

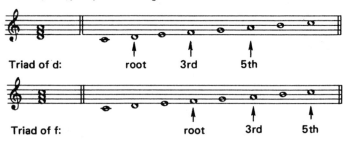

Degrees of the Major and Minor Scales: notes classified according to their position in the scale. These classifications hold true for both major and minor scales.

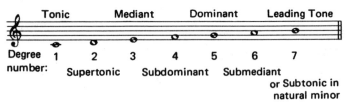

Triads of the Major and Minor Scales: the quality and position of a triad are represented by Roman numerals. An uppercase numeral representes a major triad; lowercase numerals are used for minor triads. For example: IV would represent a major triad based on the 4th degree of a scale. Alterations in these two basic types of triads are indicated with slashes. An uppercase numeral with a downward slash indicates an augmented triad; diminished triads are represented by a lowercase numeral with an upward slash.

Major Scale triad qualities:

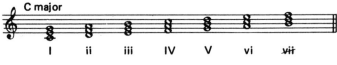

Minor Scale triad qualities:

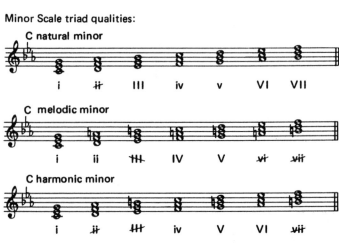

Consonance: any harmonic structure which does not require resolution; containing only imperfect intervals of unisons, 4ths, 5ths, or octaves.

Dissonance: any harmonic structure which requires resolution; containing the dissonant intervals of 2nds, 7ths, or any augmented or diminished interval. In functional harmony, any note that forms a 4th with the bass is considered a dissonance.

Diatonic scale: an arrangement of consecutive half- and whole-steps in alphabetical sequence, using all seven letter names. For example: a major or minor scale.

Chromaticism: the addition of altered tones to the basic diatonic scale. For example: in E major, B is a diatonic note; B , B , B , etc., are chromatic.

Non-harmonic tones: tones used melodically (linearly) which are not part of the harmonic (vertical) structure. The following are the most common non-harmonic tones.

A *passing tone:* (abbreviation, *P.T.*) connects two chord tones conjunctly.

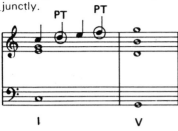

A *suspension* (abbreviated, *S.*) is a chord tone that is held across a change of harmony, becomes dissonant, and resolves by downward conjunct motion to a different, consonant chord tone. The most common suspenseions are the 4—3, 7—6, 9—8, and 2—3 (in the bass).

An *appoggiatura:* (abbreviation, *App.*) usually occurs a step above the chord tone to which it resolves. It must occur on a strong beat and resolve by descending motion. It is often written as a grace note.

Retardation: describes delayed resolution (suspension) which may resolve in either direction.

Lower neighboring tones: (abbreviation *L.N.T.*) embellish a chord tone by moving downward in conjunct motion and then back.

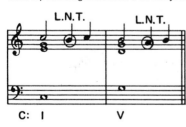

Upper neighboring tones: (abbreviation *U.N.T.*) embellish a chord tone by moving up by step and then back.

Anticipation: (abbreviation, **Ant.**) is created by using a non-harmonic tone that precedes the chord to which it belongs. Rhythmically, it falls on a weak beat and is usually shorter than the note it anticipates.

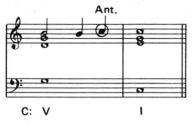

C: V   I

Echappee: (or **escape tone**) is a non-harmonic tone which is approached by step and resolves by leap in the opposite direction.

C: IV   I

Cambioto: non-harmonic tones which leave the harmonic tone by leap and resolve by step in the opposite direction.

C: IV   I   V   I

Four-part harmony: In its simplest form, functional harmony consists of triads. A four-part texture is created when one note of the triad is doubles; usually the root of the chord. Each part is named after vocal ranges. From highest to lowest they are soprano, alto, tenor, bass.

Disposition: refers to the vertical spacing between notes of a triad. If the spacing between tenor and soprano is an octave or less, the chord is in **close** position. If there is more than an octave between tenor and soprano, the chord is in **open** position.

The six dispositions for a root-position triad with the root doubled are:

Close Position   Open Position

The distance between any adjacent voices should not be more than an octave except between tenor and bass.

Rules of Voice-Leading

Melodic motion
   conjunctly (stepwise motion) or
   disjunctly (making leaps larger than a 2nd).

For **Conjunct motion,** major and minor 2nds are the smoothest and most desirable intervals.

In consonant harmonic progressions, **Disjunct motion** in the voices uses major and minor 3rds, perfect 4ths and 5ths, major and minor 6ths, and the octave.

Dissonant intervals such as the augmented 2nd, augmented 4th or diminished 5th are very rarely used, and 7ths may be used only in dissonant harmony.

The diminished 5th (or augmented 4th) may be used in the soprano voice only when approaching the leading tone.

Doublings

1. In four-part writing, one of the notes of the triad must be doubled. The note in question is usually doubled at the octave or second octave; occasionally it must be doubled at the unison. Most frequently the root is doubled, less often the 3rd is doubled, and in special cases the 5th is doubled.

2. If a note other than the root must be doubled, it is usually best to stress one of the most important degrees of the scale, i.e. the tonic, subdominant, or dominant.

3. Tendency tones—tones that demand resolution—are never doubled. This includes the leading tone which functions as a tendency tone in V or vii.

4. Tones which form a dissonance with the bass should not be doubled.

5. Occasionally the 5th of a triad may be omitted where the root is tripled. This is done sometimes in final cadences on the tonic triad.

6. In the progression V to vi in major, and V to VI in minor, the 3rd of the vi triad must be doubled to allow for resolution of the leading tone and to avoid parallel octaves.

Parallel Octaves and 5ths

Parallel octaves and 5ths are never used in functional harmony and should be avoided. This includes consecutive octaves and 5ths created by contrary motion.

Direct Octaves and 5ths

1. Direct octaves and 5ths (octaves or 5ths reached by similar motion) are limited to inner voices.

2. Direct octaves in outer voices may be used only if the soprano moves stepwise and the progression is IV—I or V—I.

3. Direct 5ths may be used between outer voices if the soprano moves stepwise.

Root-Position Progressions

Progressions by Perfect 5th and Perfect 4th
In functional harmony, the strongest progression in a key is that of a descending 5th (or ascending 4th). The next strongest progression is that of a descending 4th (or ascending 5th).

In progressions in which the bass moves by a 5th, the harmonization can:
1. keep the common tone and move the other voices in contrary motion to the bass; or
2. moves all voices to the nearest notes of the next chord in stepwise similar motion to the bass.

In progressions in which the bass moves by 4ths, the harmonization can:
1. keep the common tone and move the other voices in similar motion to the bass; or
2. move all three voices in contrary motion to the bass.

Progressions by 3rd
A somewhat weaker progression is that by 3rd (in either direction). When the bass moved by 3rd, the harmonization can:
1. keep two common tones and move the other in contrary motion to the bass;

2. move all three voices in contrary motion to the bass;

3. move a voice in contrary or similar motion to the bass where a note other than the root is doubled.

Progressions by 2nd:

This is the weakest possible root-position progression.

1. The most logical voice-leading is to move all voices in contrary motion to the bass.

2. The exception to this is the progression V–vi (see the last example of Part II).

3. Another exception is the progression V–IV (V-iv) which produces a cross relation when the leading tone is in the soprano.

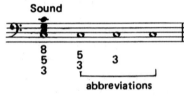

C: V   IV

The tritone is accentuated in a cross relation.

Figured Bass Harmonization

A given bass note to be harmonized with a root position triad can be represented by the numbers written below the given bass note.

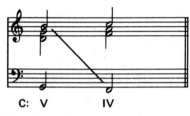

Sound

8
5
3   5   3
         3

abbreviations

The numbers represent the intervals above the bass note that are to be used in the harmonization. No number below the given bass note means it is in root position.

Progressions Involving Inversions

Inversions: are chords with any component other than the root in the bass. Inversions are used to give greater melodic freedom to the bassline while maintaining strong functional progressions (those based on 4ths or 5ths).

6ths Chords: are triads in first inversion; i.e. the 3rd of the triad is in the bass. In figured bass this is represented by the number $\frac{6}{3}$ or 6.

Sound

6
3   6

Stepwise Motion in the Bass

By using alternating root position and first inversion triads, it is possible to have melodic conjunct motion in the bass.

C: I   ii   I 6   vii 6   I

Sequences

One of the most common sequential harmonizations uses the alternation of root-position triads and first-inversion triads.

Circle of Fifths

C: I 6   vii 6   iii   vi 6   ii   V   I

In this harmonization, the sequential motion in all voices is created by doubling the 3rd in the first-inversion triads and the root in root-position triads.

$^6_4$ Chords

These are triads in second inversion—the 5th of the triad is in the bass. Since any voice which creates the interval of a 4th with the bass is considered a dissonance, they are used only in special cases.

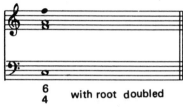

$^6_4$ with root doubled

The *neighboring tone* $^6_4$ is often found as an embellishment of the authentic cadence (see Part V). Two voices remain stationary while two other voices move to their neighboring tones and back.

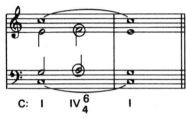

C: I   IV$^6_4$ I

In this example it is proper to double the 5th of the IV chord.

The neighboring tone $^6_4$ can also be found as an embellishment of the bass line. In the first example three voices move to their neighboring tones, while in the second only two voices are moving.

G: I   V$^6_4$ I

G: I   V   I

The *passing tone* $^6_4$ is found when the bass moves from a root-position triad to a first inversion of the same triad, or vice versa. In this case the 5th of the chord is always doubled since it does not function harmonically, but melodically.

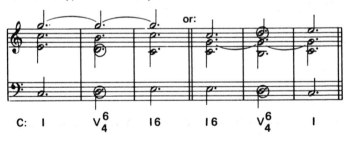

C: I   V$^6_4$ I6   I6   V$^6_4$ I

The *appoggiatura* $^6_4$ (or *cadential* $^6_4$) appears on the tonic triad and has a doubled fifth. It prepares a root-position dominant chord by having two of its voices resolve downward. It is a common cadential formula found in music from the 18th century onward.

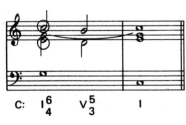

C: I$^6_4$ V$^5_3$ I

The appoggiatura $\frac{6}{4}$ is often embellished by adding a 4—3 suspension (see Part I, Non-Harmonic Tones). By delaying the reolution of the appoggiatura an even greater feeling of tension is created before the final tonic triad.

Harmonic Function

Harmonic Function
The relationship between chords is what creates the feeling of motion in music.

Tonic Function
The tonic triad does not create a feeling of motion in music. The tonic triad in and of itself is static, essentially serving as a point of departure and arrival.

Dominant function
Dominants create the effect of motion in music by being a point of tension. For example, the progression V—I creates the effect of tension then rest, and is tht most powerful harmonic force in music.

The dominant triad demands resolution because it contains the leading tone, which is a tendency tone within a key. Any chord containing the leading tone, such as vii, may function as a dominant substitution and also requires resolution.

In minor, the v chord contains the lowered leading tone (subtonic) which has no harmonic force and usually leads away from the tonic rather than toward it.

Supertonic function
The supertonic being a 5th away from the dominant, serves as its preparation. This has the effect of creating more *tension* before the final required resolution. For example, ii—V—I equals tension—tension—rest.

Certain chords—such as IV—may serve as supertonic substitutions if they prepare the dominant chord.

Plagal function (or Neighboring Tone function)
The IV (iv) chord is usually very weak since it is reached by a descending 5th or ascending 4th from the tonic. For this reason, it is felt as a departure from the tonic rather than an approach to it. The most distinguishing aspect of the plagal function is its use as an extension of the authentic cadence (see Part VI).

Any chord that uses neighboring tones to connect with another chord may be considered a plagal function.

The chords vi, iii, and vii do not function independently. They operate as strong functions only when connected by a strong 5th (descending 5th or ascending 4th).

In moving away from the tonic by a strong 5th, all the chords are reached. This is called a *circular progression.* The strength of the functions increases as they move toward the tonic.

a minor

i   iv VII   III VI   ♯   V   i

Cadences

Cadence: a point at which music rests; a progression of usually two chords at the end of a phrase that gives the effect of resolution.

Authentic Cadence (V—I)
Any cadence which contains the progression V—I is considered to be an authentic cadence.

The *Perfect authentic cadence* is an authentic cadence in which both chords are in root position and the tonic note is in the soprano in the final chord.

An *Imperfect authentic cadence* is an authentic cadence in which the 3rd or 5th of the final chord is in the soprano.

Plagal cadence (IV—I or iv—i)
Thie is the most relaxed type of cadence, and is used mostly as an ornament to the authentic cadence.

Deceptive cadence (V—vi or V—VI)
This is a cadence in wich an expectation for the usual resolution of the dominant is set up and then avoided. This is accomplished by having the vi chord substitute for the tonic triad.

Interrupted cadence
This involves a sudden and unexpected resolution of the dominant chord on something other than a vi chord.

Half cadence (ii—V, ii-V, II—V, iv—V)
This is a momentary rest on the dominant chord which will eventually be resolved to the tonic.

Dissonant Dominant Harmony

7th Chords

Dominant 7th Chord
The 7th, when added to the dominant triad, increases the amount of tension it creates and makes its function more apparent. In some cases the relationship between triads may not be perfectly clear. With the added 7th, the point of arrival is obvious.

The first example can be explained as V—I in C, I—IV in G, VII—III in A, or III—VI in E.

With the added 7th in the second example, there is a definite feeling of C major.

Since the dominant 7th chord consists of four notes, there are three possible inversions. In figured bass, they are represented by the following figures. (The numbers in parentheses are optional):

Root Position	1st Inversion	2nd Inversion	3rd Inversion
7	6	(6)	(6)
(5)	5	4	4
(3)	(3)	3	2

In dominant 7th chords, the root may be omitted, making the chord diminished—(appearing as vii but analyzed as V°7 because of its function.

Treatment of the 7th

1. It must resolve in stepwise descending motion.
2. It cannot be doubled.
3. It may be approached by conjunct or disjunct motion.

In progressions V7 —I (V7 —I), one of the two chords will have to be incomplete in order to provide proper voice-leadings. If the V7 is incomplete, it is best to omit the 5th which is not an essential component. The root then would be doubled.

Secondary Dominants

The dominant 7th chord can appear as a dominant to any degree of the scale. These can be used to strengthen certain progressions and are considered borrowings from other keys. In these cases the 7th usually resolves downward by step.

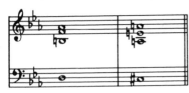

Complete Dominant 9th Chords

A complete dominant 9th chord have five components; this includes the 7th.

In four-part writing, the form omitting the 5th is considered a complete 9th chord.

Treatment of the 9th

1. The 5th is the least essential component and is omitted.
2. A 9th chord may resolve directly to the tonic. The 9th of the triad can resolve before the tonic by descending to the dominant note.
3. No special treatment of the 9th is necessary. It may remain unresolved.
4. The disposition is important. The 9th must be at least a 9th above the root. The 9th also must be placed at least a 7th above the leading tone.

Incomplete Dominant 9th Chords

These are analyzed in progressions as V°9, meaning that the root is omitted. Since the root of the chord is often omitted, no standard figuration is used.

1. the 9th must be placed at least a 7th above the leading tone.
2. in minor, the V°9 is a diminished 7th chord (all minor 3rds) in which any of the four components may serve as a leading tone. This is easily used to shift suddenly to distant keys.

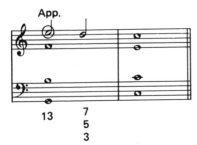

Dominant 13th Chords

The main feature of dominant 13th chords is an ornament (appoggiatura) to the 5th of the dominant 7th chord. The resulting harmony became standardized in cadential formulas of the 19th century.

Dissonant Supertonic Harmony

Supertonic 7th Chords
1. A 7th may be added to the supertonic triad as with the dominant triad. All voice-leadings and doublings are identical.
2. A supertonic 7th without the root is analyzed as ii°7 or II°7.
3. the most important alteration of the supertonic chord is raising the 3rd, making it major (II7). In essence it functions as a dominant but often resolves to another dissonance (that of the dominant chord): II−7V7.
4. The Major II7 in treatment is identical to the V7.

Supertonic 9th Chords
1. The Major II7 in treatment is identical to the V7.

Supertonic 9th Chords
1. 9ths are most freuently added when the chord is major (II) and is functioning as a preparation to the dominant.
2. Supertonic 9ths are treated as dominant 9ths.

Supertonic 11th Chords
The supertonic 11th is created by multiple appoggiaturas. In most cases the 3rd and 7th are omitted. Often the 3rd and 9th are omitted.

Supertonic Substitutes
Sevenths may freely be added to VI and vi when serving as supertonic substitutes.

Chromatically Raised Supertonics
1. Often the root of a supertonic is raised, making the triad diminished (ii). With an added 7th (ii7), the chord becomes a diminished 7th chord and may be handled as the V°9.
2. The supertonic substitute vi may also be altered in a similar manner to vi and vi7, giving greater freedom in modulating to distant keys.

Chords with an Altered 5th

Dominant Chords with Raised 5th
V$\sharp$5 is used as a chromatic passing tone.

C: I   V$\sharp$5—of→IV

V$\sharp^7_{\sharp5}$ is used with double chromatic passing tones.

C: V 7   V$^{\sharp7}_{\sharp5}$ I

A chromatically raised component must resolve in that direction. Raised 5ths and 7ths must resolve upwardly by semitone.

Dominant Chords with Lowered 5ths
The lowered 5th most often appears in the bass.

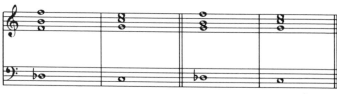

C: V$^{°7}_{\flat5}$ V$^{7}_{\flat5}$ I

Counterpoint
Counterpoint
Counterpoint
Counterpoint
Counterpoint
Counterpoint
Counterpoint
Counterpoint
Counterpoint
Counterpoint
Counterpoint
Counterpoint
Counterpoint
Counterpoint
Counterpoint
Counterpoint
Counterpoint
Counterpoint
Counterpoint
Counterpoint
Counterpoint
Counterpoint
Counterpoint

Counterpoint
Counterpoint
Counterpoint
Counterpoint
Counterpoint
Counterpoint
Counterpoint
Counterpoint
Counterpoint
Counterpoint
Counterpoint
Counterpoint
Counterpoint
Counterpoint
Counterpoint
Counterpoint
Counterpoint
Counterpoint
Counterpoint
Counterpoint
Counterpoint
Counterpoint
Counterpoint
Counterpoint

Definitions

Counterpoint: Note heads in the Renaissance were shaped as small diamonds which were considered to be "points" on the staff indicating pitch with various modifications to indicate duration. Any notes played against the original notes (or points) with adherence to strict rules are said to be "counter" to "point," or that which is played "against" the original notes.

Cantus Firmus: "Fixed song," an established melody, usually a Gregorian chant, to which the counterpoint is set.

Motion: the direction in which a note in the melody progresses to the note which follows.

Types of Melodic Motion *(movement in one voice):*

1. Stationary — same tones

2. Conjunct — melody moves stepwise

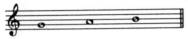

3. Disjunct — leaps of a third or larger

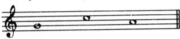

Types of Harmonic Motion *(movement in two or more parts):*

1. Parallel — both voices moving in the same direction, each by the same interval.

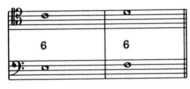

2. Similar — both voices moving in the same direction but by different intervals.

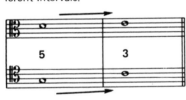

3. Oblique — one voice moving and the other remaining stationary.

4. Contrary — both voices moving in opposite directions.

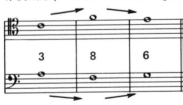

Consonance: the harmonic intervals of a unison 3rd, 5th, 6th and an octave.

Of these, the unison, 5th and octave are said to be perfect; the 3rd and 6th are said to be imperfect.

	1 (unison)	3	5	6	8 (octave)
	Perfect	Imperfect	Perfect	Imperfect	Perfect

Dissonance: the harmonic intervals of a 2nd, 4th, 7th, and 9th.

	2	4	7	9

Tritone: the interval of an augmented 4th (or diminished 5th).

	dim.♯5	aug.4	aug.4

This interval, referred to as *Diabolus in Musica,* is strictly avoided.

Species: this refers to the five types of rhythmic relationships between the *cantus firmus* and the *counterpoint,* to which the strictest of rules apply.

Accented Beat: the strong beat of a measure.

Unaccented Beat: the weak beat of a measure.

In *second species,* the first half of the measure is considered accented and the second half unaccented. In *third species,* the first and third beats of the measure are considered accented and the second and fourth beats of the measure unaccented.

Modes: species counterpoint uses the six Renaissance modes:

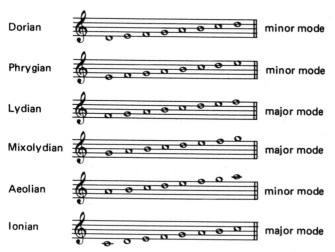

Dorian — minor mode
Phrygian — minor mode
Lydian — major mode
Mixolydian — major mode
Aeolian — minor mode
Ionian — major mode

Vocal Ranges: clefs are employed in the practice of strict counterpoint.

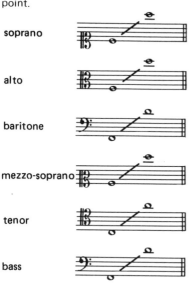

soprano

alto

baritone

mezzo-soprano

tenor

bass

Basic Rules of Melodic Motion:

The intervals which are allowed:
1. Major and minor 2nds
2. Major and minor 3rds
3. Perfect 4ths, perfect 5ths, and octaves
4. Occasionally, a minor 6th in ascending motion only

The highest or lowest tone is best placed in the middle or toward the end of the phrase.

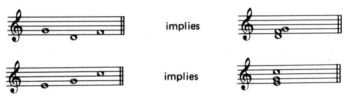

Leaps of a third or more are generally followed by stepwise motion in the opposite direction.

More than one skip in the same direction is rarely used.

Outlines of triads and 7th chords are forbidden because of their harmonic implications.

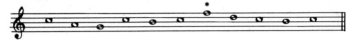

Avoid the following:

1. Repetitions

2. Sequences

3. Palindromes

The cantus firmus must begin on the tonic note. The next to last note must be the 2nd degree of the mode (one step above the tonic).

Never used in melodic motion:

1. Tritone (diminished 5th or augmented 4th)

2. Leap of a 7th

3. Leaps larger than an octave

Cadences:

1. The last note of the counterpoint must be the tonic.

2. The next to last note of the counterpoint must be the 7th degree of the scale (a semi-tone below the tonic) except in the *phrygian* mode, where the 7th degree is a whole step below the tonic.

3. In the *dorian, mixolydian* and *aeolian* modes, the 7th degree is raised at the cadence (e.g. C♯ instead of C♮).

In the *aeolian* mode, the 6th degree is raised to avoid the augmented 2nd if stepwise motion is used.

 *instead of*

4. The leading tone at the cadence should be approached by con-junct motion or by descending 3rd.

First Species

Note against note. (One note of counterpoint to each note of cantus firmus.)

Basic Rules of Harmonic Motion:

1. Use only consonant intervals (unison, 3rd, 5th, 6th, and octave).

2. The interval between the voices should not be larger than a 12th.

3. Begin the counterpoint on a perfect consonance (unison, 5th, or octave).

4. End the counterpoint on a unison or octave.

5. When the counterpoint is below the cantus firmus, begin on an octave or unison.

6. Parallel octaves or 5ths are never used.
Consecutive octaves or 5ths are never used.

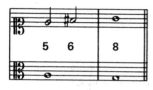

7. More than three steps in parallel motion (3rds, 6ths, 10ths) is forbidden.

8. Perfect consonances (octaves, unisons, 5ths, 12ths) approached by similar motion are never used.

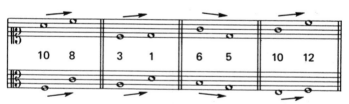

9. Avoid crossing of voices. If necessary, a few notes may be crossed.

10. Avoid false relation of tritones (i.e., the first note of one voice creates an augmented 4th with the second note of the other voice).

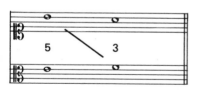

Counterpoint in First Species

11. Contrary motion is the most desirable.

Second Species

Two notes against one (two notes of counterpoint to each note of cantus firmus)

Basic Rules of Melodic Motion:

1. The first measure of counterpoint must contain a half rest at the beginning, or accented part, of the measure.

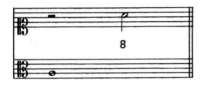

2. The last measure must be a whole note.

3. The next to the last measure may be either two half notes or a whole note.

4. Stationary motion (repetition of a note) should be avoided.

Basic Rules of Harmonic Motion:

1. Dissonances may appear on the second half (unaccented part) of the measure.

Major and minor 2nds, perfect 4ths, tritones, major and minor 7ths, major and minor 9ths, and perfect 11ths are used.

2. The first beat (accented part) of each measure must be a consonance.

3. The unaccented part may be a:

consonance

dissonance as a passing tone

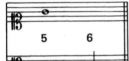

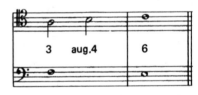

dissonance by lowering the counterpoint one step

4. Beware of parallel octaves or 5ths coming from the unaccented part of the measure.

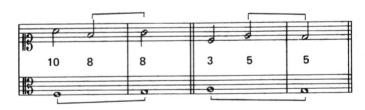

5. Beware of creating parallel octaves or 5ths in consecutive measures.

Counterpoint in Second Species

Third Species

Four notes of counterpoint to one note of cantus firmus (quarter notes against whole notes).

Basic Rules of Melodic Motion:

1. The first measure may begin with a quarter rest followed by three quarter notes.

2. The last measure must be a whole note.

3. The next to the last measure may contain four quarter notes or two half notes (according to second species counterpoint.)

4. The first and third beats of the measure are considered accented. The second and fourth beats are unaccented.

5. Ascending leaps from accented beats are to be avoided.

6. Parallel unisons, octaves or 5ths should not be used moving from the third or fourth beat to the first beat of the next measure .

7. Occasionally octaves at the beginning of consecutive measures are used.

Basic Rules of Harmonic Motion:

1. Dissonances may be used on the unaccented part (second and fourth beats) of the measure. They may be passing tones or lower adjacent tones.

2. The *cambiata* is a five note melodic figure in which the dissonant note must be approached by conjunct motion, followed by a leap of a 3rd in the same direction and left by conjunct motion in the opposite direction.

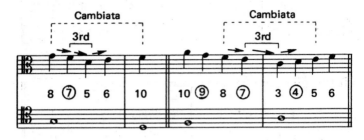

The cambiata may begin on the first or the third beat of the measure.

3. A passing tone on an accented beat can be used occasionally when approaching a cadence. The other three beats must be consonances.

whole note

4. One dissonance should never follow another.

5. Unisons are permissible at times, but should never be used on the first quarter note of the measure. They are usually left by conjunct motion in the opposite direction.

6. Parallel octaves and 5ths should not be used.

7. It is permissible to use consecutive octaves and 5ths between accented beats *only* when approaching a cadence.

8. Voice crossings of no more than two or three notes can be used.

9. In this species, successive 3rds, 6ths, and 10ths may be used with greater freedom. Avoid the same interval at the beginning of several successive measures.

Counterpoint in Third Species

Johann Joseph Fux
(1660-1741)

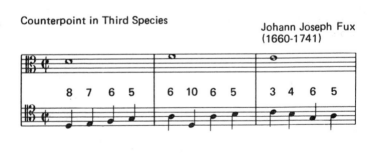

5 4 3 5   3 6 10 3   3 5 4 3   1

Fourth Species

Similar to first species except that the counterpoint note is often delayed for half the measure and tied over to form the first part of the next measure. This species, also called *syncopation,* makes use of the prepared dissonance called the *suspension.*

Basic Rules of Melodic and Harmonic Motion:

1. Suspensions must be prepared; that is, they are tied over the measure from a consonance.

8   6   ⑦   6   8

2. All suspensions must resolve to a consonance in a descending conjunct (stepwise) motion.

3. The only suspensions used in a counterpoint *above* the cantus firmus are the 4 to 3 suspension (11 to 10) and the 7 to 6 suspension.

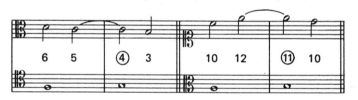

6   5   ④   3   10   12   ⑪   10

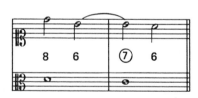

8   6   ⑦   6

4. The only suspension used in a counterpoint *below* the cantus firmus is the 2 to 3 (9 to 10).

6   5   ②   3   6   8   ⑨   10

5. The first measure of counterpoint must begin with a half rest.

6. The first note of the counterpoint must be a perfect consonance.

8

5

7. The leading tone at a cadence must be approached by a suspension.

8. Parallel or consecutive octaves and 5ths should be avoided.

9. When suspensions are not possible, the syncopation may be continued by ties over the measure.

10. Voice crossings are occasionally allowed but for no more than one measure.

Counterpoint in Fourth Species

Luigi Cherubini
(1760-1842)

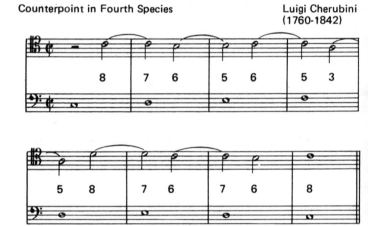

Fifth Species

Florid counterpoint. An integration of all preceding species. In this species, eighth notes and dotted halves may be used.

Basic Rules for Rhythm:

1. Whole notes or half notes may be tied over the bar line but only to a note of equal duration or less.

2. Eighth notes may be used in some instances, mainly approaching cadences but only on the second or fourth beats of the measure.

Basic Rules of Melodic Motion:

1. Strong scale motion and melodic curve are desirable.

2. Repetitions of notes may not be used.

Basic Rules of Harmonic Motion:

1. When two eighth notes are used, either one may be dissonant but both must be used conjunctively.

2. Dissonances may be used as they are used in the other four species.

3. An accented passing tone may be used on the third beat if it is preceded by a half note or larger.

4. When approaching a cadence, an upper adjacent tone may be used.

5. Suspensions may be ornamented with:

two eighth notes

or an anticipation

Counterpoint in Fifth Species

Orchestration
Orchestration
Orchestration
Orchestration
Orchestration
Orchestration
Orchestration
Orchestration
Orchestration
Orchestration
Orchestration
Orchestration
Orchestration
Orchestration
Orchestration
Orchestration
Orchestration
Orchestration
Orchestration
Orchestration
Orchestration
Orchestration
Orchestration
Orchestration

Orchestration
Orchestration
Orchestration
Orchestration
Orchestration
Orchestration
Orchestration
Orchestration
Orchestration
Orchestration
Orchestration
Orchestration
Orchestration
Orchestration
Orchestration
Orchestration
Orchestration
Orchestration
Orchestration
Orchestration
Orchestration
Orchestration
Orchestration

Families and Ranges of Instruments

Woodwinds
Flutes: *Piccolo, Flute* (soprano), *Alto Flute* (in G), and *Bass Flute* have a written range:

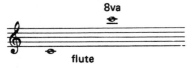

The piccolo sounds an octave above its written range:

The flute sounds as written;
also flute sounds a perfect 4th below its written range and the bass flute sounds an octave lower than written.

Oboe: Sounds as written:

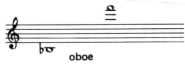

Although the *English horn*
has the same written range, it is in concert F and sounds a perfect 5th lower than written.

Clarinets: *E Piccolo, Soprano Clarinets* (in B♭ and A), *E♭ Alto,* *B♭ Bass,* and *Contrabass* (in E♭) have a wide written range:

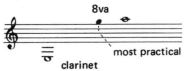

The clarinets are all transposing instruments. Piccolo in E♭ sounds a minor 3rd above written pitch; the B♭ clarinet sounds a major 2nd lower, the A clarinet sounds a minor 3rd below, the E♭ alto sounds a major 6th below; the B♭ bass sounds a major 9th below; and the E♭ contra, an octave and a major 6th below.

Saxophones
Written range:

The *B♭ Soprano Saxophone* sounds a major
2nd lower than written; the *E♭ Alto* sounds a major 6th below; the *B♭ Tenor* sounds a major 9th below; the *E♭ Baritone* sounds an octave and major 6th below; and the BB bass sounds two octaves and a major 2nd below. The bass sax is rarely used. The *Bassoon* and *Contrabassoon* are written:

The contrabassoon sounds an octave lower than its written range.

Brass: The *French horn* (in F) is written:

and sounds a perfect 5th below. The **Trumpets** are in many different keys; the most common is B♭. The range of brass instruments depends on the player. The best players may have a written range:

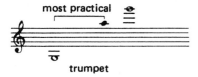

trumpet

sounding a major 2nd below. The **Tenor** and **Bass Trombone** both sound as written. Tenor:

tenor trombone

Bass:

8va bass

trombone

The most commonly used **Tuba** is the BB♭, written an octave above sound:

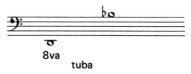

8va

tuba

The **percussion** section of the orchestra contains everything from **Drums, Cymbals, Mallet Instruments** and assorted **Traps** (special-effect instruments) to the **Harp** and **Keyboard Instruments.** The staff setup with drums and cymbals varies; however, the lines and spaces are always designated and follow from high to low on the staff as they would sound. The common drums (high to low) are: **Snare, Tenor, Tom-toms** (high, medium, low), and **Bass drum.** **Cymbals** also come in many sizes. Drum parts are notated in either bass clef or with a clef without a pitch designation.

percussion

Mallet Instruments The **Vibraphone** has metal bars with resonators that allow for the tones to sustain. Its range is:

vibraphone

The **Marimba** has wooden bars that create a unique and colorful sound; however, the tones do not sustain. It has a very wide range:

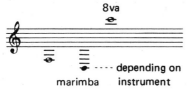

marimba   instrument

The **Xylophone** has a very bright timbre and sounds an octave above written:

xylophone

The **Harp** is a diatonically tuned instrument on which one must shift foot pedals in order to play accidentals. Its range:

8va

is set up on a grand staff as a piano.

(The piano's range:)

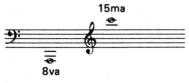

The *Guitar* sounds
an octave below its written pitch. It has 6 strings tuned a perfect 4th
apart except for the 2nd and 3rd strings, which have a major 3rd
between them:

guitar tuning

The range of most guitars extends to the C an octave and a major 6th
above the pitch of the first (high) string.

Strings: The *Violin, Cello, Violoncello (Cello),* and *Double Bass*
each have four strings. The strings of the violin, viola and cello are a
perfect 5th apart; the bass strings are a perfect 4th apart. The *Violin:*

violin

Viola:

viola

Cello:

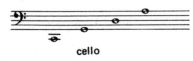

cello

The *Double Bass* sounds an octave below its written pitch

double bass

In general, the notes of the very high register can be difficult to lo-
cate and tune. For this reason, passages written higher than an octave and a major 6th above the first string are to be avoided.

Transposition

The concept of transposition is quite simple. An instrument based
on pitch other than concert pitch (C) lies at a certain interval from
concert pitch: if the pitch is in E♭, then the transposition interval is
either a minor 3rd above or a major 6th below. This interval determines the pitch at which music for the instrument must be written
to sound concert pitch. Example: the clarinet in B is a major 2nd
below concert pitch (B♭ is a major 2nd below C); therefore, the
clarinet must be written up a major 2nd to sound at concert pitch.

The register of the instrument determines whether the interval is
above or below concert pitch. Example: the E piccolo clarinet and
the E alto saxophone are both pitched in the same key and are
written in the same registers but they transpose differently. The
the concert range of the E♭ piccolo clarinet is

E♭ piccolo clarinet

the E♭ alto saxophone is

saxophone

The E♭ piccolo clarinet's lowest
sounding pitch is a minor 3rd below concert sound. The E♮ alto saxophone's lowest sounding pitch is a major 6th below its lowest written pitch; therefore, it is written a major 6th above concert sound.
The process can be applied to all transposing instruments.

Standard Combinations

The orchestrator should have an understanding of the standard
instrumental combinations which appear throughout music history.
There were several types of ensembles which were popular during
these periods and it is easy to see how they affected the growth of
chamber repertoire.

We can follow the development of orchestration and style through
the evolution of the orchestra. Classicists, such as Haydn (1732-
1809) wrote for an orchestra which consisted of two flutes, two
oboes, two bassoons, two french horns, timpani, two sections of
violins, one section of violas, celli, and basses (which doubled the
cello line an octave below). Haydn used trumpets occasionally and
clarinets appear in two late symphonies. Mozart (1756-1791) in-
corporated clarinets into the standard orchestra. Beethoven bridged
the gap between the classical orchestra and the romantic orchestra
with his middle to late symphonies. He would occasionally add a
piccolo, contrabassoon, two additional horns, trombones, percussion, and independent lines for the double bass. Wagner, Mahler,
and Strauss enlarged the orchestra in the 19th century to include
as many as eighteen first violins, sixteen second violins, twelve
violas, ten celli, eight double basses, two harps, three flutes, one
piccolo, three oboes, one English horn, three clarinets, one bass
clarinet, three bassoons, one double bassoon, six horns (sometimes
eight), four trumpets, four trombones, one tuba, four kettledrums,
one glockenspiel, one tenor drum, one bass drum, chimes, xylophones, celesta, cymbals, etc. The orchestra still continues to
change and grow with present day composers.

Standard instrumental combinations are also drawn from within
the family groups. The **woodwinds** divide into combinations of
trios, quartets, quintets, etc. The trio consists of flute, oboe, and
clarinet; or flute, oboe, and bassoon; or oboe, clarinet, and bassoon.
The standard quartet is flute, oboe, clarinet, and bassoon. The standard quintet adds the french horn to the woodwind quartet (flute,
oboe, clarinet, french horn, and bassoon). The sound of the woodwind quintet is versatile as the horn complements and colors the
woodwinds beautifully.

The **brass** usually divide into trios, quartets, and quintets. Trios of
trumpet, french horn, and trombone; quartets of two trumpets and
two trombones; and quintets of two trumpets, french horn, and two
trombones (or one trombone and a tuba).

The standard **string ensemble** is the **string quartet.** Two violins play
independent lines and are complemented by a viola and a cello.
Occasionally, the quartet can be expanded to a quintet with the
addition of one viola or cello; or a sextet, by adding two violas or
two celli. Some composers have written for an octet which is a
double string quartet. The trio usually consists of a violin, viola, and
cello; however, some works can be arranged for two violins and viola.

There is a variety of standard mixed ensembles. Duos for piano with
another instrument. Trios: piano trios consisting of piano, violin,
and cello, or piano with a woodwind and a string instrument; quartets through nonets (nine) for piano and string or wind ensembles,
or a combination of strings and woodwinds, including french horn.

There are many varieties of wind ensembles, all of which have very
rich, sonorous textures. The basic large wind combination consists
of two flutes, two oboes, two clarinets, two bassoons, and two
french horns. The basic ensemble can be expanded by adding additional pairs of any instrument; from the simplest addition of two
french horns to the large Straussian wind groups incorporating
extra pairs of the related instruments such as piccolos, E♭ clarinets,
bass clarinets, English horns, contrabassoons, etc.

In jazz and popular idioms, there are different standard combinations. The "rhythm section," consisting of piano, bass, and drums
(sometimes with guitar), is the backbone to all small and large ensembles. The dance band or big band is made up of four sections:
three to five saxophones—alto (a), tenor (t), and baritone (b); a,a,
t,t; a,a,t,b; a,t,t,b; a,a,t,t,b—two to four trumpets, two to four trombones (including bass trombone), and a rhythm section. Most saxophone players "double" on flute or clarinet, or both. The small
ensembles are groups that range from as little as one horn (woodwind or brass) with a rhythm section to a small big band.

Many popular and show ensembles also include string sections. They are in smaller and sometimes different proportions from that of the standard orchestra since a different type of sound blend is required

Characteristics of Instruments

A major part of orchestration is being able to understand the characteristics of instruments. The orchestration is more likely to sound right if the instruments are arranged so that the piece may be played idiomatically.

The **woodwinds** are extremely facile and can accommodate the most difficult passages; however, their limitations become greater in the ensemble.

The *flute* prefers its upper register in most cases, as its lower register projects poorly. It is an instrument that can be combined well with any other, although it is easily covered in the low and middle registers. Sometimes that problem can be resolved by raising the flute line an octave; the harmony doesn't sound altered by the octave displacement and the quality is often appropriate. Flutes voice well together at any interval, but it is best to voice them close.

The *oboe* is an expressive instrument in classical and popular music, but has not yet caught on in jazz. It does not have the agility of the flute and clarinet, and the lower and uppermost registers are not consistent in intonation and dynamics unless the player has control and a good embouchure. However, it blends well in wind and mixed ensembles. The oboe voices best in close harmony, octave, or unison scoring as it has a highly concentrated tone. It is also easy to articulate very fast passages.

The *clarinet* has an extraordinary range, agility and flexibility, and can produce many tonal shadings. It is comfortable in many different idioms and blends well with all instruments. The clarinet sounds well harmonizing in any type of voicing and large intervalic leaps are characteristic. Of the auxiliary clarinets, the bass clarinet is used more frequently than the piccolo and it responds more slowly, technically, than the others.

The *saxophones* are somewhat limited in range and use. Although they have been "typecast" as jazz instruments, they prove remarkably versatile in the hands of an experienced classical player. Their technical potential is almost as great as the clarinet's. The instruments themselves are very different. The *soprano* is much like the oboe in sound, does not have any difficult registers and is used predominantly as a solo instrument, not a sectional one. However, it voices well above the other saxophones. The *alto* is the lead instrument of the section; it is adept at executing very fast passages and maintaining a light, crisp sound. The alto also blends well with the trumpet. The *tenor* is full bodied and capable of supporting and blending with any instrument. As a solo instrument, it has a considerable expressive range and is a favorite among accomplished saxophone players. Despite its attributes, it remains difficult to play well; the acoustic design makes for difficulty in controlling the evenness of tone and intonation in the very low and high registers. For sectional or harmonic writing it is best to use those registers sparingly. The *baritone* is the bottom of the standard sax section. It has a tremendous dynamic range in the low and middle ranges but has difficulty projecting well in its high register. The baritone voices very well with low brass and woodwinds, and is a good choice for the bass wind in small ensembles.

The *bassoon* has a distinctive, dark timbre which projects very well in concert but somehow gets lost among the other instruments in recording. The bassoon blends well with all instruments. Its upper register adds color to the upper woodwinds and its middle and lower registers voice well with the lower woodwinds and brass.

The **brass** instruments present an entirely different set of possibilities for the orchestrator. They are capable of producing sweet sounds as well as sharp, brassy, and bright sounds. They are all capable of executing fast passages with good, clean articulation and have a repertoire of special effects, such as shakes, scoops, glissandi, etc. The *french horn* has a mellow sound that blends with woodwinds, brass, and strings. Unison or harmonized horn sections are extremely beautiful and effective. The horn actually has a wide range, but does not execute fast passages or wide intervalic leaps very well. It is not necessarily a loud instrument and its tone spreads (unfocused); writing for two or more horns in unison will focus and enhance the sound. The horn can stop a note, which means that the player uses his hand as a mute to make the timbre very small, intense, and brittle. (Stopping is notated with a + above the note and cancelled with a o which means open.)

The **trumpets** and **cornets** (two different instruments that recently have been used interchangeably) sound best in their middle ranges. They have the least difficulty executing technical passages and can accommodate the widest intervalic leaps within that register. The high register depends upon the player's own abilities. The trumpet blends the best with other brass and saxophones. Combination with woodwinds tends to bring out the brightness of its tone and combination with strings tends to bring out its mellowness. The trumpet should be voiced as the lead, in both these groups as it is the strongest and most prominent in color. The trumpet player is usually equipped with a variety of mutes. Mutes not only quiet the sound but change the tone color as well. The **straight mute** produces a bright and tinny sound and is good for crisp, sharp, staccato passages. The **harmon mute** has a beautifully veiled sound that is good for harmonized passages backing up a vocal or instrumental solo. The **cup mute** softens the sound and brings out a slightly bright edge to the tone. The **trombone** is not capable of very fast step-wise intervalic passages in its low to middle registers but is quite agile in its middle to upper. The upper register is not that easily developed as the mouthpiece has a large rim and cup and the trombone has a large bore. The sound is very large and full bodied and it can play smooth, legato lines beautifully.

The **tuba** has a spread-out sound because of its very large conical bore and large mouthpiece. This unfocused quality has as many advantages as it has disadvantages. On the bottom of the ensemble the tuba adds great dimension to the quality of the sound and will smooth the harmonies of the instruments above it. Otherwise it has a slow response in technical passages.

The **strings** have a vibrant and concentrated sound and are capable of producing a wide variety of colors by employing different bowing and fingering techniques. As a section, strings blend the best. The sound is generally uniform from the violin to the double bass. They are all extremely expressive instruments.

The **violin** has the most intense tone and is the most agile. It is capable of playing passages with great speed and large intervalic leaps are not a problem unless they involve the very high register. Its projection is surpassed only by the cello.

The **viola** has a uniquely beautiful tone—it is warm and rich and can be haunting and elegiac. Unfortunately, it does not project very well. It can negotiate difficult technical passages but requires music of subtlety to be most effective.

The **cello** has a very big, rich, and dark tone quality to its sound. It projects the best of all the strings and it is the only one that can support a line as one, in a large string ensemble. The cello has a very large range and great technical facility.

The **double bass** is an odd instrument; its tone tends to spread like the tuba's. However, it doesn't project very well and has poor technical responsiveness. Yet in a section, it adds great dimension to the harmony and color of an orchestration due to its range and overtones.

There are many bowing techniques that the orchestrator can take advantage of: **sul ponticello, sul tasto, pizzicatto, col legno, spiccato, jete, ricochet,** etc. Harmonics and multiple stops (two to four notes played at one time) are also coloristic and technical devices string players use.

Combining Instruments

The music may dictate certain colors and timbres, yet there is always more than one way to orchestrate a given piece. Within an ensemble, the individual instruments serve specific functions which are complemented by the players' abilities. The orchestrator must consider the musical character of each instrument and how it interacts in the ensemble.

Basic principles can be learned from the logic of the standard combination. Many are comprised of instruments from one family and have a homogenous quality. In a sense, it is impossible to make an orchestration error this way; all one must remember are the ranges of the individual instruments. Most scores are set up to illustrate their positions: the **string quartet** is arranged with the violins on top, the viola in the middle, and the cello on the bottom; they would be voiced the same way.

For more specific circumstances it is important to orchestrate idiomatically. An orchestrator must assess the character of the music. A simple harmony works differently between different sections: a root position major triad voiced by a violin, viola, and cello; or trumpet, french horn, and trombone; or flute, oboe, and clarinet—all have entirely different effects. Some combinations that theoretically work can be quite impractical.

In the example above (a triad voiced with different groups), the strings and brass both work well; however, the quality of the sound differs so much that they would not be used in the same context. Surprisingly, the woodwinds are not desirable at all because the sound does not focus and define a character. If a simple harmony is affected so greatly by a few simple combinations, then an entire phrase or composition becomes music on the basis of how well the orchestration expresses it.

Two important aspects of combining instruments are voicing: the position of the notes (in what registers they sound) in a chord—and voice leading: the motion of the notes from one chord to another. There are three basic voicing categories: closed position, when all the chord tones are adjacent; semi-open position, when chord tones are not adjacent but within close proximity of each other; and open position, when chord tones are not close together. It is necessary to have a knowledge of counterpoint and harmony to satisfy the different voicing preference for each situation.

The idiom is important in determining what combinations and voicings are most desirable.

During the classical period, violins were most often voiced by harmonizing them in 3rds and octaves. This practice became the model for voicing all melody instruments, especially the pairs of woodwinds found in the classical orchestra. The lower strings generally harmonized accompaniment patterns, which put the viola as a subordinate voice to their of the upper parts, if support were needed, or to the celli, which established the bass. As harmony became more chromatic and more parts were needed to create richer sonorities, the strings were divided. A single section might harmonize in close parallel motion allowing for some counterpoint in another section. Parts for the middle and lower strings, now independent (especially the basses), became more melodic and contrapuntal. With the growth of the orchestra, the string section also expanded. Careful contrapuntal writing with strings makes for a larger and plusher sound. Only when the strings are in their high register is it important to keep the sections in unison. The high woodwinds often double the strings to color the texture.

Wind ensembles as basic as two flutes, two oboes, two clarinets, two bassoons, four french horns, and tuba, have a beautiful range of sonorities. The flutes and the oboes generally share the higher register in closed voice, parallel, or chorale style voicing. The clarinet usually maintains the middle range between the oboes and the horns; oboes scored below the clarinets sound very weak. The horns, as in all horn sections in orchestral scoring, are written first and third horn high and fourth horn low. The upper horns in any wind ensemble prefer to be above the bassoon, unless the bassoon is involved with the harmony and texture of the upper winds (it blends well with the oboe and clarinet). The horn blends well with the upper woodwinds and is also in its most comfortable register; in its low register it is less flexible and tends to sound dense.

Brass ensembles of trumpets, horns, trombones, and tuba have an immense sound, not only in volume, but in dimension. The brass, when in large groups of four to a section, have overlapping ranges and generally sound best in closed or semi-open voicing.

The mixed ensemble of various sizes became most prominent in the 20th century. As classical and romantic harmony became stretched to chromaticism and music without tonal centers, the timbre and color of individual notes became just as important as preserving a blend for tonal balance. The contrapuntal nature of this music requires that the orhcestrator be sensitive to the blend of the ensemble and the identity of line. This leads to ensembles that are grouped according to function in the music rather than similarity of family, although that may coincide.

The popular idioms have maintained the more traditional approach, since they are traditionally based on a harmonic style. The dance band or big band consisting of five saxophones, two altos, two tenors, and a baritone, four trumpets, four trombones, and rhythm section (piano, bass, and drums) has fairly standard voicing principles. All the sections are versatile in their own way. It is characteristic for the saxophones to play long melodic passages in unison, closed position, or semi-open position voicing in parallel motion. Proper semi-open voicing is achieved by opening the lead alto a little from the section and doubling—the melody in the second tenor an octave below. Semi-open is a little less intense and fuller than closed voicing. In slower tempi, like ballads, open voicing is desirable; it creates a feeling of great space. It is important to try to conciliate the tempo with the voicing; an open tempo will complement a more relaxed rhythm. Cluster voicing consists of a strongly dissonant group of notes lying close together. It produces an interesting sound without losing richness. Saxophones have the ability to blend so well that they can change voicings through a passage without weakening the texture. Most saxophone players double on either clarinet or flutes or both. Clarinet lead over sax voices well in perfect 4ths with a 3rd between the two lower parts.

The *trumpets* are at their best when voiced in closed position, unison, or octaves. They are instruments with a high and intense sound. Voicing the trumpets in open position will tend to contradict the timbre and will result in a sound which is clumsy. Trumpet players also play better in tune in closed position.

It is important to keep the trumpets in a comfortable range, not too high, because it is tiring for the player. Most trumpet players double on flugelhorn. It has a much larger bore, and as a result, a mellower sound.

The *trombone* sounds equally well in all voicings. It is a sonorous instrument and is excellent for solo roles. A lead trombone can maintain a strong high register but it is best not to tax it.

Since the 1950s, 60s and 70s, the french horn and tuba have been included in jazz ensembles. Both are good for harmonic and supportive roles and both blend well in the jazz ensemble. The rhythm section takes care of itself. It is important to designate the chord changes in each bar with rhythm for the piano and the bass. The drummer needs the basic rhythm and cues for the piano, bass and the band periodically. It is also helpful to give them cues for major events in the music—changes in dynamics or tempo, time changes, stops, etc.—they are the ones who set them. Scoring for *strings* in the popular idiom is quite different from scoring in the classical. Strings are usually used in recordings of popular music and occasionally as backup for a jazz artist. Each situation requires special attention. An orchestrator will often divide the violins into three groups and score with celli on the bottom. Violas usually do not respond well in this idiom while the high celli and low violins lend a great amount of resonance. It is also better to have an extra violin in the lead section. There should never be less than three violins on a part. One is very weak, two do not blend well and tend to be out of tune, while three or more blend beautifully. The double bass does not project well in concert, but is strong in a recording situation.

Setting Up the Score

All scores follow the orchestral layout: woodwinds from high to low on top, followed by brass (french horns above trumpets), harp, piano, percussion and strings. If the score is for a smaller group, the arrangement is the same, omitting the unnecessary instruments. The two types of scores are the concert score and the transposed score. Transposed scores (all parts written as they would be for each player) are generally preferred over concert scores (all parts written as they sound).

Suggestions for the Aspiring Orchestrator

Counterpoint and harmony are as essential to the orchestrator as an understanding of the instruments.

Listening is one of the best ways to learn. Listen carefully to styles of music, composers, arrangers, and musicians. Try to distinguish what makes them different and what makes them similar. In the classical idiom, listen to the orchestral and chamber works of Bach, Mozart, Beethoven, Berlioz, Brahms, Wagner, Mahler, Richard Strauss, Ravel, Debussy, and Stravinsky. In the jazz idiom, the bands of Louis Armstrong, Benny Goodman, Duke Ellington, Charlie Parker and Dizzy Gillespie, Stan Kenton, Miles Davis and Gil Evans, Gerry Mulligan, and Thad Jones and Mel Lewis. In addition, listen to rock, film scores, and theater music.

Although reading scores may not be easy at first, there is a lot of information in them. Here are a few things to do:

- Begin by identifying the melodic lines.
- Identify the harmonic lines and/or the counterpoint.
- Figure out the harmonic motion of the music.
- After you begin to understand the music, pick out the combinations of instruments that appear to be doing similar things.

Bibliography

Berlioz, Hector. *A Treatise on Modern Instrumentation and Orchestration.* Saint Claire Shores, MI: Scholarly Press, 1976.
Garcia, Russell. *Professional Arranger Composer.* Hollywood: Criterion Music Corporation, 1954.
Hedick, Brook. *Music Theory: Glossary.* New York: Acorn Music Press, 1981.
Joseph, Stuart. *Percussion Instruments Chart.* New York: Acorn Music Press, 1980.
Murphy, Brenda. *Bassoon Fingering Chart.* New York: Acorn Music Press, 1979.
———. *Clarinet Fingering Chart.* New York: Acorn Music Press, 1979.
———. *Flute Fingering Chart.* New York: Acorn Music Press, 1979.
———. *Horn Fingering Chart.* New York: Acorn Music Press, 1979.
———. *Music Theory: Rudiments.* New York: Acorn Music Press, 1980.
———. *Oboe Fingering Chart.* New York: Acorn Music Press, 1979.
———. *Saxophone Fingering Chart.* New York: Acorn Music Press, 1979.
———. *Trombone Fingering Chart.* New York: Acorn Music Press, 1979.
———. *Trumpet Fingering Chart.* New York: Acorn Music Press, 1979.
———. *Tuba Fingering Chart.* New York: Acorn Music Press, 1979.
Piston, Walter. *Orchestration.* New York: W.W. Norton & Company, Inc., 1955.
Ricigliano, Daniel. *Popular and Jazz Harmony.* New York: Donato Music Publishing Company, 1967.
Rimsky-Korsakov, Nikolay. *Principles of Orchestration: With Musical Examples Drawn from His Own Works, 2 Volumes in 1.* Steinberg, Maximillian, ed. Magnolia, MA: Peter Smith, Publisher.
Sebesky, Don. *The Contemporary Arranger.* Sherman Oaks, CA: Alfred Publishing Company, 1975.
Zeitlin, Ralph. *Music Theory: Counterpoint.* New York: Acorn Music Press, 1981.
———. *Music Theory: Harmony.* New York: Acorn Music Press, 1981.

51

Glossary

Glossary

Glossary

A capella: vocal music written and/or performed without instrumental accompaniment.

Absolute music: abstract music; music disassociated from literary or poetic images (as opposed to program music).

Absolute pitch: see pitch

Accent: the emphasis through either rhythm or dynamics of a note (<).

Accidental: the symbol for an alteration in pitch that is not included in the key signature; a flat (♭) lowers a pitch one semitone, a sharp (♯) raises it one semitone, and a natural (♮) dictates that the note remain unaltered.

Air, Ayre: a simple melody.

Aerophones: of the four general acoustic classifications of instruments, the one that relies on an enclosed column of air to generate sound: i.e. woodwinds, brass instruments. (To compare, see *chordophones, idiophones,* and *membranophones.*)

Alberti bass: piano accompaniment figures for the left hand that consist of broken chords.

Alla breve: a tempo marking ( ) indicating quick duple time.

Allemande: a dance movement in moderate $\frac{4}{4}$ time, often used to open a classical suite.

Alto: 1. see *voices, range of* 2. usually the second highest part in a four-part chorus.

Appoggiatura: an accented, nonharmonic tone that usually resolves in a downward, stepwise movement to an adjacent tone included in the structure of the chord.

Aria: a song, usually of some complexity and associated with opera or oratorio, for solo voice and instrumental accompaniment.

Arpeggio: the notes of a chord played in succession instead of simultaneously.

Atonal: not in any key; without tonality or a traditional tonal center.

Augmented: see intervals.

Badinage, badinerie: French for playfulness, banter; title for a quick, dance-like piece used in 18th century suites.

Ballad: a narrative, strophic song; often a folk song or based on folkloric themes.

Ballade: usually a composition based on dramatic, fanciful or romantic subject matter. Plural: balladen.

Ballet: a theatrical performance of substantial length relying chiefly on dance and music rather than singing or the spoken word to convey its narrative.

Band: an instrumental group composed chiefly of wind or percussion instruments.

Bar: synonym for *measure.*

Barcarolle: boating song, generally associated with Venetian gondoliers, in $\frac{6}{8}$.

Barform: a German term for the musical scheme of A A B.

Barline: the vertical line drawn through the staff to delineate measures or other divisions in the music.

Baroque: Dates: 1600-1750; the musical period immediately following the Renaissance. Composers associated with the Baroque are Monteverde, G. Gabrielli, Caccini (early Baroque); Purcell, Lully, Vivaldi, J.S. Bach, and Handel (middle to late Baroque). Styles and forms associated with the Baroque are the rise of monody, opera, oratorio, passion, cantata; the use of thoroughbass and counterpoint; the concerto grosso, prelude, fugue, suite, chorale, passacaglia and toccata.

Bass: 1. see *voices, range of* 2. the lowest part in a four-part chorus.

Beat: 1. a regular rhythmic pulse; the basic unit of musical time. 2. the actual physical movement used to communicate this pulse.

Bel canto: a vocal ideal and technique of the 18th century emphasizing finely cultivated lyric tone instead of dramaticism; usually associated with the vocal demands found in the operas of Bellini, Donizetti, Mozart, etc.

Bagatelle: a short, light piece usually for piano.

Binary form: describes the musical scheme A B and is the historical basis for sonata form.

Bourree: a dance movement in quick double-time usually beginning with an upbeat.

Brace: (Accolade in French, Klammer in German): the vertical line combined with a bracket that joins different staves.

Brass instruments: instruments made of brass or other metals played through a cup-or funnel-shaped mouthpiece; the lips of the player vibrate to generate the sound; e.g. trumpets, tubas, french horns, bugles, etc.

Cadence: a progression of usually two chords at the end of a phrase that gives the effect of resolution.

Cadenza: an extended solo musical passage, often improvised and usually at the end of a composition, that constitutes an interruption in the flow of the piece and allows the soloist to display his virtuosity.

Canon: a polyphonic composition where each instrument (or voice) has the same melodic line but begins it at different times.

Cantata: an extended composite choral work with orchestral accompaniment. The text is usually based on a secular or religious narrative.

Cantus firmus: a pre-existing melody used as a basis for a contrapuntal or polyphonic composition.

Capriccio: a light, lively piece.

Chaconne: a piece in slow triple meter in which a given theme is continually repeated in the bass.

Chamber music: music originally intended for performance in a room as opposed to a hall. Unlike orchestral music, chamber music generally has one player to a part.

Chant: see *Plainsong.*

Choir: a group of singers, especially in a place of worship (as opposed to the secular *chorus*).

Chorale: four-part pieces based on traditional hymn tunes of the German Protestant church.

Chord: the simultaneous sounding of three or more tones.

Chordophones: of the four general acoustic classifications of instruments, the one that relies on the vibration of a string or strings to produce sound. (To compare, see *aerophones, idiophones,* and *membranophones.*)

Chorus: 1. a group of singers 2. music written for such a group 3. the extended refrain of a song.

Chromatic: adjective used in reference to intervals outside a major or minor scale and also for stepwise movements by semitones.

Chromatic scale: a scale consisting of twelve degrees that ascends and descends by semitones.

Classicism: Dates: 1770-1830 (Viennese classicism); more a style and ideal than an actual period. Classicism is usually contrasted with romanticism due to its focus on clarity, balance, stability, structure, and traditionalism. Composers associated with classicism are Haydn, Mozart, Beethoven, and Shubert. Forms developed during the classical period were the symphony, concerto, sonata, divertimento, and the string quartet.

Clef: a symbol placed at the beginning of the staff to indicate the pitch of the notes.

treble or   bass or
G clef   F clef   soprano clef   alto clef   tenor clef

Coda: a section added to a piece to conclude it that is not considered to be a part of its basic compositional structure.

Codetta: a short coda.

Coloratura: a florid musical style for soprano most common in operatic arias of the 18th and 19th centuries relying on trills and rapid, virtuostic passages.

Common time: $\frac{4}{4}$ meter, also written 𝄴

Concerto: a composition for solo instruments and orchestra, each with equally important integrated parts.

Concerto grosso: a composition for a small group of instruments (a concertino) that plays parts which complement and contrast with those played by a larger group of instruments.

Consonance, Dissonance: terms used to describe the relationship between pitches. Consonant intervals (e.g. octaves, fifths) are said to sound pleasing, stable, or agreeable. Dissonant intervals (e.g. seconds, sevenths) are said to sound rough, discordant, or disagreeable.

Contralto: see ***alto.***

Corrente, Courante: a dance, generally in three; often used as a movement in some suites.

Counterpoint: the technique of combining two different, independent melodies to create one logical, musical texture.

Cyclic, cyclical: 1. of a musical form containing several movements 2. of a composition where a musical theme occurs in more than one movement.

Degree: the classification of a note in terms of its position in a scale.

Descant: 1. an additional, usually florid, part (sometimes improvised) sung or played above the normal melody and harmony of a hymn 2. an early term for the highest voice in part music and/or the instrument playing that part.

Development: the section of a piece where the originally stated themes are combined, expanded, modified.

Diatonic: of or relating to major keys, minor keys, or scales in which chromatic tones are excluded.

Diminished: see ***interval.***

Dissonance: see ***consonance.***

Divertimento: a light instrumental work for a small musical group in several movements; popular during the latter half of the 18th century; considered chamber rather than orchestral music.

Dominant: 1. the fifth degree of a diatonic scale 2. the chord built on the fifth degree (V chord=dominant; V7=dominant seventh).

Drone: a long sustained tone or tones, usually low in pitch.

Duet: 1. a composition for two performers where each part is of equal importance. 2. an ensemble of two.

Duo: see ***duet.***

Duple meter: see ***meter.***

Duplet: a pair of notes to be played in the time of three: e.g.

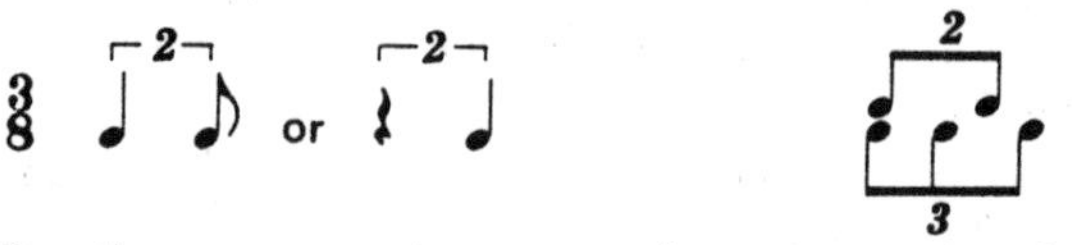

Duration: an acoustic term used to characterize the length of a sound.

Dynamics: degrees of loudness or softness in music.

Ecossaise: a quick dance in $\frac{2}{4}$, not Scotch in origin, but descended instead from the English country dance.

Eighth note: ♪ two or more eighth notes may be beamed together: ♫ (see ***time values***).

Eighth rest: 𝄾 (see ***time values***).

Encore: the performance of an extra piece, or the repetition of a piece in concert brought on by the demands of an enthusiastic audience.

Enharmonic: sounds that differ in notation but not in pitch, e.g. G## and A .

Ensemble: 1. a group of performers 2. the quality of teamwork during a performance or rehearsal 3. in opera, a piece for more than two singers, or for soloists and chorus.

Entr'acte: music to be performed during the intermission of a play, opera, etc.

Etude: a piece intended to aid a student in developing his instrumental ability.

Exposition: 1. the initial segment of a piece in which the main themes are stated (precedes development) 2. the first section of sonata form.

Expressionism: Dates: (roughly) 1910-1930; a term borrowed from art used to categorize certain trends and ideals in music that occurred predominantly in Austria and Germany. It implies a calculated turning away from expressionism and a focus on expressing the subconscious self. Although not the most useful term, composers associated with expressionism are Schoenberg, Webern, Berg, and occasionally Hindemith.

Fandango: a Spanish/South American dance in triple time traditionally accompanied by a guitar and castanets.

Fanfare: a short melody for trumpets used as a herald of a significant social ceremony.

Fantasia, Fantaisie, Fantasie, Fantasy: a fanciful, free piece where the composer's imagination takes precedence over traditional structure.

Fermata: pause (⌢) ⌢

Figured bass: see *thorough bass.*

Finale: 1. the last movement of a piece comprised of several movements 2. the last piece in an act of an opera.

Flat: see *accidentals.*

Fugue: a form of imitative counterpoint marked by the imitation of the theme by each individual voice in close succession. The initial theme reappears throughout the piece repeatedly in all voices.

Galliard: a lively dance of the 16th century usually in a quick three.

Gavotte: a French dance in moderate $\frac{4}{4}$ time, marked by phrases that usually begin and end in the middle of a measure.

Gigue: a French dance used as a movement in baroque suites: similar in style to a jig.

Glissando: the technique or effect of a rapid, uninterrupted passage up or down the scale.

Grace note: an ornamentive note set in small type; not accounted for in the original time signature but subtracted from the time value of the note that it either follows or precedes.

Grand staff: the treble and bass staves braced together.

Gregorian chant: liturgical chant of the Roman Catholic church named after Pope (St.) Gregory I (590-604) during whose reign (and possibly sponsorship) the chants were arranged and codified.

Ground bass: (also *basso ostinato*): a short four to eight measure) phrase which is continually repeated as a bass line to complement the melodies and harmonies of the upper parts.

Half note: ♩ (see *time values*).

Half rest: (see *time values*).

Half step: (see *semitone*).

Harmonic: of or relating to harmony.

Harmonic minor: see *minor scale.*

Harmonics: a term for the acoustic phenomena that result from the fact that there are no pure tones, and that a pitch is a composite of many overtones (or partials). These are not heard as distinctly as the tone for which the pitch is named (the lowest tone or fundamental) but serve to establish the perceived quality (or *timbre* of the sound).

Harmony: the simultaneous sounding of tones in a way that is musically significant.

Hornpipe: a primarily English dance popular during the 16th through 19th centuries. It originally had three beats to a measure, and later was used as a melody to which sailors performed a solo dance.

Hymn: a song of praise or adoration to a deity.

Idiophones: of the four acoustic classifications of instruments, the one that could most easily be considered percussion instruments. Idiophones are shaken, struck or rubbed. (To compare, see *aerophones, chordophones,* and *membranophones.*)

Imitation: a compositional technique common in polyphonic writing in which a melody is restated in close succession by the other voices.

Imperfect: see *perfect.*

Impressionism: a French school of painting in the late 19th and 20th centuries, represented in music by the composers Debussy (1862-1918) and Ravel (1875-1937). The internal structure of the music is subtle, hinting rather than stating; a succession of colors taking the place of dynamic development. Unresolved dissonances, quasi-modal harmonies, consonant or dissonant chords used in parallel motion, and some use of the whole tone scale gives this music its vague and intangible quality.

Improvise: to perform extemporaneously without the benefit or hindrance of music memorized or written.

Incidental music: music, usually instrumental, written to be performed during a play.

Intermezzo: 1. a short, lyric concert piece 2. a light theatrical entertainment performed between the acts of a play or opera 3. an entr'acte.

Interval: the distance in pitch between two tones simultaneous or successive. An interval is measured according to the number of degrees in the diatonic scale that it encompasses.

Intonation: the quality of a performer's execution of accurate pitch; playing in tune.

Inversion: 1. the alteration of a chord or an interval by placing any pitch other than the root in the bass 2. the alteration of a melody by "turning it upside down"; the intervals involved would remain the same, but would ascend where they once descended and vice versa.

Jig: a dance usually in $\frac{6}{8}$ or $\frac{12}{8}$, closely associated with English comedians of the 16th and 17th centuries; often used as a final movement in 18th century suites.

Key: the predominant note, scale or tonal center of a piece.

Keynote: the tonic.

Key signature: the sharps and flats that appear at the beginning of each staff to indicate the key of a piece.

Landler: a German dance in three.

Leading tone: the seventh degree of the scale.

Legato: to be performed smoothly, without interruption.

Leger lines, ledger lines: the short lines used to extend the range of a staff.

Libretto: the text for an opera.

Madrigal: term for a style of polyphonic unaccompanied vocal music, the text of which was drawn chiefly from courtly poetry. There were two distinct eras during which the madrigal enjoyed great popularity and refinement: in Italy from approximately 1520 to 1600; and in England from approximately 1590 to 1640.

Major; Minor: terms used to qualify the tonality of intervals, triads, chords, scales, and keys.

Major scale: a series of eight pitches with consecutive letter names (the eighth being an octave repetition of the first) arranged in a fixed pattern of whole and half steps: W W ½ W W W ½. A major scale can be built from any pitch as long as the whole- and half-step relationships remain the same.

Mass: 1. the principal service of the Roman Catholic church 2. the musical choral setting of this liturgy comprised of five sections: Kyrie, Gloria, Credo, Sanctus, and Agnus Dei.

Measure: a regular arrangement of groups of beats delineated by bar lines.

Mediant: a name given to the third degree of the scale. It precedes the *subdominant* and follows the *supertonic* degrees.

Medieval: approximated dates: 500-1540; the musical period preceding the Renaissance and historically divided into several periods and styles: Gregorian chant, Ars Antiqua, Ars Nova, and the Burgundian School. Although much medievel music remains anonymous, some of the known composers associated with this early music are: Leonin, Perotin, Bernart de Ventadorn, Machault, Landini, Dufay, and Binchois. Forms associated with medieval music are chant, organum, troubadour songs, laude, ballata, caccia, and virelai.

Medley: a series of tunes performed in succession.

Melody: a succession of notes perceived as a musical entity.

Membranophones: of the four general acoustic classifications of instruments, the category under which drums would fall; percussion instruments that rely on the vibration of a stretched skin to generate sound. (To compare, see *aerophones, chordophones,* and *idiophones.*)

Metre, Meter: the basic and regular grouping of beats into measures. When there are two basic time units in a measure ($\frac{2}{2}, \frac{2}{4}, \frac{4}{4}$, etc.) one speaks of duple metre. When there are three units in a measure ($\frac{3}{2}, \frac{3}{4}, \frac{3}{8}$, etc.) one refers to triple metre.

Metronome: a device used to indicate exact tempo and capable of sounding an adjustable number of beats per measure.

Middle Ages: see *Medieval music.*

Middle C: the C found in the middle of the *Grand staff.*

Minor: see *major.*

Minor scale: a series of eight pitches with consecutive letter names (the eighth being the octave repetition of the first) arranged in a fixed pattern of whole and half steps. There are three basic minor scales:

Natural minor: W ½ W W ½ W W

Harmonic minor: W ½ W W ½ W ½ ½; it is the raised seventh degree that differentiates the harmonic minor from the natural minor.

Melodic minor: ascending—W ½ W W W W ½: descending—W W ½-W W ½ W.

Minuet: a popular French court dance in triple time commonly used as a third movement in the classical sonata, symphony, string quartet, etc.

Modal: of or relating to modes.

Modes: the general term for the organization of a series of pitches into a coherent and fixed system. The most commonly encountered are the so-called church modes. These are constructed, using the tones of the C Major scale, as follows:

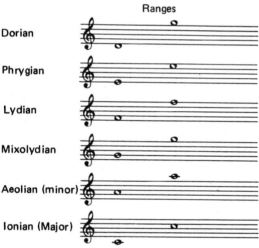

Modulation: harmonic movement from one key to another during the course of a composition.

Monody: music for one voice.

Monophony: music comprised of a single line of melody; one of the oldest types of music.

Motet: an important form of early polyphonic choral composition originally in Latin and designed to be performed in the Catholic service. Motets were a popular compositional concern for approximately 500 years (1250-1750) and as a result went through several significant developmental phases.

Motive, Motif: the smallest unit of a musical idea.

Movement: a complete, self-contained division within a large composition.

Musette: a type of gavotte with a drone that suggests the sound of 17th and 18th century French bagpipes of the same name.

Mute: an apparatus for muffling or softening an instrument.

Nationalism: a concern shared by several musical epochs denoting a concern for using musical ideas that suggest supposed national characteristics. It is used particularly in reference to certain 19th century composers such as Grieg, Mussorgsky, Smetana, and Liszt.

Natural: see *accidentals.*

Neo-classicism: a concern of some 20th century composers that began in the 1920s (notably with Stravinsky and Hindemith) characterized by the desire to infuse contemporary music with classical techniques and forms.

Neumes: one of the earliest forms of music notation; used primarily for plainsong.

Nocturne: a short lyrical piece for the piano in one movement.

Note: a written symbol that represents the pitch and duration of a musical sound.

Obbligato: 1. a compulsory and important part that must not be omitted 2. occasionally (and common in modern music), means the opposite of the above; an optional accompanying part.

Octave: the interval between two tones that share the same letter name; twelve semitones.

Octet: 1. a composition for eight instruments or voices 2. an ensemble of eight.

Opera: a theatrical performance where the characters sing throughout and in which the accompanying music constitutes a principal element having its own unity.

Opera buffa: a comic opera.

Opera comique: opera of the 19th century with spoken dialogue connecting the music.

Operetta: a light theatrical piece with spoken dialogue, music, and often dancing; more simple and popular in its style than opera.

Opus: a term that precedes a number indicating the chronological position of a composer's published piece. If an opus consists of more than one piece, it is subdivided further. For example, Brahms Op. 63, No. 4 indicates that it is the fourth song in Brahms's sixty-third published work.

Oratorio: an extended work for solo voices, chorus, and orchestra. Although the text is dramatic in nature, it is intended for performance without scenery, costumes, or action.

Orchestra: a large instrumental ensemble traditionally comprised of strings, woodwinds, brass, and percussion sections.

Orchestration: the art of writing or arranging for an orchestra, band, chamber ensemble, etc.

Ornamentation: the art of embellishing a melody with auxiliary notes. Ornaments can be indicated in the music or improvised by the performer.

Ostinato: a continually repeated melodic phrase or rhythmic figure.

Overtone: name for any of the tones in the harmonic series except the original.

Overture: instrumental work intended to precede an opera, oratorio, or play; usually incorporating themes from the body of the work.

Parallel motion: two or more moving voices maintaining a fixed intervallic relationship.

Part: 1. in orchestral or chamber music, the music for a particular instrument or voice 2. any one voice in a given ensemble.

Partials: overtones in the harmonic series of a tone.

Passacaglia; Passacaille: a piece in a moderate three in which a given theme is continually repeated in either the treble or the bass voices. (Compare to *chaconne.*)

Passage: a short section of a piece.

Passing tone: a nonharmonic tone which stands between two harmonic tones and is approached and left stepwise in the same direction.

Passion: a musical setting of the biblical events surrounding the death of Christ. Usually intended for performance in a church the week before Easter.

Pavan, Pavane: a slow, stately court dance of Spanish origin popular in the early 16th century.

Pentatonic scale: a scale comprised of only five tones, the octave being reached at the sixth degree. Although numerous pentatonic scales can exist theoretically, the degree relationship created by the scale played on the five black keys of the piano (beginning on C) is the most common.

Percussion instruments: generic name for instruments played by striking a resonating surface (see *idiophones* and *membranophones.*) The piano and celeste are technically percussion instruments; others are: xylophones, drums, marimbas, cymbals, glockenspiels, etc.

Perfect: a term used to describe the intervals of a fourth, fifth, and octave when they are unaltered, i.e. not augmented or diminished (imperfect).

Period: a short, natural melodic division; usually two phrases.

Phrase: the musical equivalent of a sentence: a complete musical idea usually ending in a cadence.

Pitch: the property that makes notes appear to sound either "low" or "high" in relation to each other. Concert or absolute pitch is the accepted standard (a = 440 vibrations per second) to which instruments are normally tuned.

Pizzicato: a direction and technique for string instruments indicating that the instrument is to be plucked rather than bowed.

Plainchant, Plainsong: early monophonic, rhythmically free liturgical music.

Polonaise: a Polish national dance of a stately nature in $\frac{3}{4}$ time.

Polyphony: music comprised of using two or more contrapuntal voices.

Polyrhythm: the use of different contrasting rhythms simultaneously; e.g.,

Polytonality: the simultaneous use of more than one tonality; (if only one other key is introduced into a composition, the correct term would be bitonality).

Prelude: 1. a piece preceding something such as a longer work or a church service 2. a short, self-contained piece.

Program music: illustrative music; music designed to interpret or create near-literal images of extra-musical ideas (opposite of abstract music).

Quality: the property ascribed to an interval, triad, chord, scale, or melody which causes it to be identified with a specific mode. For example, the interval E to G has a minor quality while the triad C E G has a major quality.

Quartet: 1. a composition for four instruments or voices 2. an ensemble of four.

Quintet: 1. a composition for five instruments or voices 2. an ensemble of five.

Quadrille: a French square dance popular in the early 19th century, composed of several different movements.

Quartet note, Quarter rest: ♩ 𝄽   see *time values.*

Range: the compass of an instrument or voice.

Recital: a public performance generally by a soloist or small ensemble.

Recapitulation: see *sonata form.*

Recitative: a composition for voice with a minimum of musical structure emphasizing speech-like rhythms. Usually used as a means of continuing a narrative in prose texts and linking one aria or chorus to another.

Refrain: lines of text and music (usually two) that are repeated at the end of each verse of a strophic song.

Relative pitch: 1. the pitch of one tone as contrasted with another (standardized) tone 2. the ability to recognize intervals or pitch relationships.

Renaissance: approximate dates: 1400-1600; the musical period immediately preceding the baroque and following the Middle Ages, the 200 years of the Renaissance produced more musical performances and compositions than in any previous age. Part of this is due to the invention of the Gutenberg press (1440) thus making printed music accessible outside a small geographic area. The Renaissance on the Continent is associated with a concern for writing pieces that were artistically satisfying as well as socially functional; common compositions were polyphonic unaccompanied vocal music in the form of masses, motets, and chansons. Composers associated with the Renaissance are Ockeghem, Josquin, Obrecht, Isaac, and Senfl.

Reprise: 1. the repetition of a theme after the development 2. the repetition of an entire piece in a musical or operetta.

Requiem: a musical setting of the Roman Catholic Mass for the dead.

Resolution: 1. the movement of a dissonant note or chord to a consonant note or chord 2. a melodic or harmonic cadence.

Rest: a symbol notating the absence of sound for a specific amount of time.

Restatement: same as recapitulation in sonata form.

Retrograde: a melody written and/or read backwards.

Rhapsody: a title common in the 19th and 20th centuries for a piece quite similar to a fantasia.

Rhythm: the aspect of music that is not concerned with pitch, but rather with the accentuation and duration of notes.

Romantic: approximate dates: 1770-1900; the period of music immediately following classicism that, while sharing forms and certain harmonic structures, eschewed the ideal of the rational as the ultimate compositional goal. Romantics placed a greater emphasis on the qualities of remoteness and strangeness (in terms of choice and treatment of material); they cherished freedom, passion, the endless pursuit of the unobtainable and saw an intimite merging of the artist's personality with his art be he composer or performer. Lieder, balladen, fantasies, rhapsodies and program music all came of age during the romantic era. Composers associated with romanticism are: Chopin, Schumann, Brahms, Wagner, Mendelssohn, and Schubert.

Rondo, Rondo form: a form often used as the final movement in classical sonatas, symphonies, concertos, etc., in which one section recurs throughout the piece. A simple rondo pattern is A B A C A-D A etc.

Root: the first degree of a triad or chord; the tone for which the triad or interval is named.

Round: a short, vocal, cyclic canon; e.g. "Three Blind Mice."

Rubato: an instruction denoting rhythmic flexibility and freedom in order to express a phrase in as "musical" a manner as possible. Often used as a noun when describing a performer's interpretive capabilities.

Sarabande: a dignified dance of the 17th and 18th centuries in a slow three.

Scale: a progression of notes downward or upward in regulated steps.

Scherzo: introduced by Beethoven to replace the minuet as the third movement of sonatas, symphonies, and quartets, it is in a lively and rapid $\frac{3}{4}$ time.

Schottische: a popular ballroom dance of the 19th century; it is similar to the polka and should not be confused with the quicker ecossaise.

Score: a notation denoting all the different parts of an ensemble where each part is arranged on different staves set under one another.

Semitone: the smallest interval in traditional western music. One-half of a whole setp, it occurs naturally between the third and fourth degrees and the seventh and eighth degrees in a diatonic major scale.

Septet: 1. a composition for seven instruments or voices 2. an ensemble of seven.

Serenade: originally open-air evening music; the most classic example is the song of a lover beneath his mistress's window.

Sextet: 1. a composition for six instruments or voices 2. an ensemble of six.

Sharp: see *accidentals.*

Solo: a piece or passage for one performer alone or with an instrument.

Sonata: a composition for solo piano or an instrument with piano accompaniment in three or four movements: 1st, Allegro; 2nd, Largo, Adagio, or Andante; 3rd, Allegro or Allegretto; and 4th, Allegro molto, Presto, or Vivace.

Sonata form; Sonata allegro form: (also *first-movement form*): a way of constructing a long piece, frequently used for single movements of a sonata, symphone, etc. Skeletally, sonata form is the division of a piece (occasionally after an introduction) into three sections: the exposition, development, and recapitulation. It can also be defined as A A B A form; A being the exposition and its repeat; B the development of themes introduced in the exposition in a different key; and the final recapitulation—A—where the exposition returns in its original key with a few modifications.

Sonatina, Sonatine: a short, "little sonata"; usually lighter in character and easier to play than most sonatas.

Song: a short vocal composition.

Soprano: 1. see *voices, range of* 2. usually the highest voice in a four-part chorus.

Sostenuto: direction for sustaining the tone of a piece or passage.

Staccato: a musical instruction that indicates a short, detached attack of a note.

Staff: the series of five lines and four spaces on which notes—indicating pitch—are written.

Stringed instruments: generic name for instruments whose sound is produced by plucking or bowing a stretched string (see *chordophones*); e.g. violins, cellos, harps, guitars, etc.

Strophic: a term borrowed from literary analysis and used when referring to songs in which the same music is repeated for each stanza of a poem (text); the opposite of through composed.

Style: a distinctive, characteristic form of expression. Style in music can be examined historically—in terms of a composer or a composition alone—or it can refer to a performer's approach to a piece, taking both his musical sensitivities and analytic sensibilities into account.

Subdominant: 1. the fourth degree of a diatonic scale 2. the chord built on the fourth degree (IV chord=subdominant).

Submediant: a name given to the sixth degree of the scale sometimes call the super dominant. It precedes the leading tone (subtonic) and follows the dominant degrees.

Subtonic: see *leading tone.*

Supertonic: a name given to the second degree of the scale. It precedes the subtonic and follows the tonic degrees.

Suite: an instrumental piece in several movements, usually centered around a basic idea implied in its title; originally refined during the baroque when each movement was based on a dance form.

Symphony: a work of substantial length for a full orchestra; can easily be considered a sonata for orchestra.

Syncopation: the deliberate misplacement of natural rhythmic accents.

Tempo: the actual speed of a composition.

Tenor: 1. see *voices, range of* 2. usually the second lowest voice in a four-part chorus.

Ternary form: term that describes the musical scheme A B A.

Theme: a motive or phrase that serves as the basis for the development of a composition or section of a composition.

Thorough bass, Figured bass: a system of musical shorthand common during the early baroque, where numbers indicating the correct chord and its inversion are placed below a bass line.

Through-composed: a term applied to songs in which new music is provided for each stanza.

Tie: a curved line connecting two adjacent notes of the same pitch, indicating that the pitch is held for the total duration of their combined time-value.

Timbre: the distinctive, characteristic quality of a sound.

Time: term used to classify basic rhythmic qualities: meter, tempo, or duration.

Time signature: the numbers that appear at the beginning of a piece indicating the number of beats or pulses in a measure (top number), and the time value of the notes that will embody that beat (bottom number).

Time value: the duration of a given note. The names of the time values that are given notes and rests derive from the fractional parts of a measure of common time.

Tonal: of music that is perceived to observe one or more specific keys.

Tonality: 1. key 2. quality.

Tone: 1. a sound of definite pitch 2. an interval of two semitones; a whole tone.

Tonic: 1. the first degree in a scale 2. the chord built on the first degree (I chord=tonic).

Transpose: to write or perform music in a key different from that in which it was written.

Guitar Compact Reference Books

Here are other great titles in this series that you will want to add to your collection:

GUITAR

The Advanced Guitar Case Chord Book
by Askold Buk

68 pp AM 80227
ISBN 0.8256.1243.8
$4.95

Prepack AM 90176
$59.40

The Advanced Guitar Case Scale Book
by Darryl Winston

48 pp AM 91462
ISBN 0.8256.1370.1
$4.95

Prepack AM 91463
$59.40

Basic Blues Guitar
by Darryl Winston

56 pp AM 91281
ISBN 0.8256.1366.3
$4.95

Prepack AM 91246
$59.40

Beginning Guitar
by Artie Traum

64 pp AM 36997
ISBN 0.8256.2332.2
$4.95

Prepack AM 86997
$59.40

Beginning Rock Guitar
by Artie Traum

48 pp AM 37292
ISBN 0.8256.2444.4
$4.95

Prepack AM 37300
$59.40

The Compact Blues Guitar Chord Reference
compiled by Len Vogler

48 pp AM 91731
ISBN 0.8256.1385.X
$4.95

Prepack AM 91732
ISBN 0.8256.1386.8
$59.40

The Compact Rock Guitar Chord Reference
compiled by Len Vogler

48pp AM 91733
ISBN 0.8256.1387.6
$4.95

Prepack AM 91734
ISBN 0.8256.1388.4
$59.40

The Original Guitar Case Scale Book
by Peter Pickow

56 pp AM 76217
ISBN 0.8256.2588.2
$4.95

Prepack AM 86217
$59.40

Rock 'n' Roll Guitar Case Chord Book
by Russ Shipton

48 pp AM 28689
ISBN 0.86001.880.6
$4.95

Prepack AM 30891
$59.40

The Original Guitar Case Chord Book
by Peter Pickow

48 pp AM 35841
ISBN 0.8256.2998.5
$4.95

Prepack AM 36138
$59.40

Tuning Your Guitar
By Donald Brosnac

AM 35858
ISBN 0.8256.2180.1
$4.95

Prepack AM 85858
$59.40

BASS GUITAR

Beginning Bass Guitar
by Peter Pickow

80 pp AM 36989
ISBN 0.8256.2332.4
$4.95
Prepack AM 86989
$59.40

Beginning Bass Scales
by Peter Pickow

48 pp AM 87482
ISBN 0.8256.1342.6
$4.95
Prepack AM 90174
$59.40

Chord Bassics
by Jonas Hellborg

80 pp AM 60138
ISBN 0.8256.1058.3
$4.95
Prepack AM 80138
$59.40

Eight more Guitar Compact Reference Books available from Music Sales:

The Alternate Tunings Guide for Guitar
Beginning Rock Guitar
Beginning Slide Guitar
D. I. Y. Guitar Repair

Guitarist's Riff Diary
Manual de Acordes Para Guitarra
The Twelve-String Guitar Guide
Using Your Guitar

For further info contact your local music dealer or call: 914-469-2271
Music Sales Corporation   •   PO Box 572   •   Chester, New York   •   10918